Samantha Limvalencia
604 715 9085

D0210377

# GROWING IN JESUS

**6 SMALL GROUP SESSIONS ON DISCIPLESHIP**

## STUDENT EDITION

# DOUG FIELDS & BRETT EASTMAN

ZONDERVAN™

GRAND RAPIDS, MICHIGAN 49530 USA

ZONDERVAN.COM/
AUTHORTRACKER

**Youth Specialties**

www.youthspecialties.com

**Youth Specialties**

*Growing in Jesus, Student Edition: Six Sessions on Discipleship*
Copyright © 2006 by Doug Fields and Brett Eastman

Youth Specialties products, 300 South Pierce Street, El Cajon, CA 92020,
are published by Zondervan, 5300 Patterson Avenue SE, Grand Rapids,
MI 49530

**Library of Congress Cataloging-in-**Publication Data

Fields, Doug, 1962-
  Growing in Jesus : 6 small group sessions on discipleship / Doug Fields
and Brett Eastman.
    p. cm. -- (Experiencing Christ together, student edition)
  ISBN-10: 0-310-26646-7 (pbk.)
  ISBN-13: 978-0-310-26646-4 (pbk.)
  1. Discipling (Christianity)--Biblical teaching. 2. Spiriutal formation-
-Biblical teaching. 3. Discipling (Christianity)--Study and teaching. 4.
Spiritual formation--Study and teaching.  I. Eastman, Brett, 1959- II.
Title.

BV4520.F49 2006
268'.433--dc22
                                                                  2005024173

Unless otherwise indicated, all Scripture quotations are taken from
the Holy Bible: New International Version (North American Edition).
Copyright © 1973, 1978, 1984 by International Bible Society. Used by
permission of Zondervan.

Some of the anecdotal illustrations in this book are true to life and are
included with the permission of the persons involved. All other illustrations
are composites of real situations, and any resemblance to people living or
dead is coincidental.

All rights reserved. No part of this publication may be reproduced, stored
in a retrieval system, or transmitted in any form or by any means—
electronic, mechanical, photocopy, recording, or any other—except for
brief quotations in printed reviews, without the prior permission of the
publisher.

Web site addresses listed in this book were current at the time of publication.
Please contact Youth Specialties via e-mail (YS@YouthSpecialties.com)
to report URLs that are no longer operational and replacement URLs if
available.

*Creative Team: Dave Urbanski, Holly Sharp, Mark Novelli, Joanne Heim,
Janie Wilkerson*
*Cover Design: Mattson Creative*
*Printed in the United States of America*

05 06 07 08 09 10 • 10 9 8 7 6 5 4 3 2 1

# ACKNOWLEDGMENTS

This series of six books couldn't have happened if there weren't some wonderful friends who chimed in on the process and added their heart and level of expertise to these pages. I need to acknowledge and thank my friends for loving God, caring for students and supporting me-especially true on this task were Amanda Maguire, Nancy Varner, Ryanne Dearden, Jana Sarti, Matt McGill and the crew at Simply Youth Ministry. I sure appreciate doing life together. Also, I'm very appreciative of Brett Eastman for asking me to do this project.

# TABLE OF CONTENTS

# INTRODUCTION: READ ME FIRST!

**Welcome to a Journey with Jesus (and Others)!**

I hope you're ready for God to do something great in your life as you use this book and connect with a few friends and a loving small group leader. The potential of this combination is incredible. The reason we know its potential is because we've heard from thousands of students who've already gone through our first series of LIFETOGETHER books and shared their stories. We've been blessed to hear that the combination of friends gathering together, books with great questions, and the Bible as a foundation have provided the ingredients for life change. As you read these words, know that you're beginning a journey that may revolutionize your life.

The following six sessions are designed to help you grow in your knowledge of Jesus and his teachings and become his devoted disciple. But growth doesn't happen alone. You need God's help and a community of people who love God, too. We've found that a great way to grow strong in Christ is in the context of a caring, spiritual community (or small group). This community is committed to doing life together—at least for a season—and will thrive when each small group member (you) focuses on Jesus as well as the others in the group.

This type of spiritual community isn't easy. It requires several things from you:

- trust
- confidentiality
- honesty
- care
- openness
- risk
- commitment to meet regularly

Anyone can meet with a few people and call it a "group," but it takes stronger commitment and desire to create a spiritual community where others can know you, love you, care for you, and give you the freedom to open up about your thoughts, doubts, and struggles—a place where you're safe to be yourself.

We've learned from the small groups that didn't work that spiritual community can't develop without honesty. Now, at first you may be tempted to show up to your small group session and sit, smile, act nicely, and never speak from your heart—but this type of superficial participation prevents true spiritual community. Please fight through this temptation and know that when you reveal who you really are, you'll contribute something unique and powerful to the group that can't occur any other way. Your honest sharing about your heart and soul will challenge other group members to do the same, and they'll likely become as honest as you are.

To help you get to this place of honesty, every session contains questions that are intended to push you to think, talk, and open your heart. They'll challenge you to expose some of your fears, hurts, and habits. Through them, I guarantee you'll experience spiritual growth and relational intimacy, and you'll build lasting, genuine friendships.

All mature Christians will tell you that God used others to impact their lives. God has a way of allowing one life to connect with another to result in richer, deeper, and more vibrant lives for both. As you go through this book (and the five others in this series), you will have the opportunity to impact someone else—and someone else will have the opportunity to impact you. You'll both become deeper, stronger followers of Jesus Christ. So get ready for some life change.

## WHO IS JESUS?

Most people have an opinion about Jesus. But many of these opinions are based on what they've heard or come up with on their own—what they'd *prefer* Jesus to be—as opposed to their own discovery of Jesus through the Bible. People believe Jesus was all kinds of things—a great teacher, a leader of a revolution, a radical with a political agenda, a gentle man with a big vision, a prophet, a spiritual person who emphasized religion. Still others believe he is who he claimed to be—God.

The Jesus of the Bible is far more compelling than most people's opinions about him. *Growing in Jesus* allows you to get to know Jesus as his first followers did. They met Jesus as Teacher, a rabbi. They came to know Jesus as Healer, Shepherd, Servant, Savior, and ultimately the One who defeated death—the risen Lord. From his first words, "Follow me," through his ministry, death, and resurrection, he kept drawing people deeper into his life.

Jesus asked his disciples to commit their lives to God's way. As you read the Bible, you'll see that God's ways weren't always easy or comfortable for the disciples to follow. But what motivated them to do what he taught was their rich experience of who he was and all he did for them. *Connecting in Jesus* will ground you in that same experience so you'll more fully desire to follow Jesus and commit to his ways—even when it's not easy or comfortable. The Jesus you're about to encounter is waiting for you to meet him, get closer to him, and commit your life to following his ways and teachings.

When you align your life with Jesus, you're in for a wild, adventurous life. It won't be without its difficulties, but it'll be a better life than you ever dreamed possible.

## WHAT YOU NEED TO KNOW ABOUT EACH OF THESE SIX SESSIONS

Each session in this study contains more material than you and your group can complete in a typical meeting of an hour or so. The key to making the most of each session is to choose which questions you'll answer and discuss and which ones you'll save for your alone time. We've tried to make it simple, so if you miss something from one meeting, you can pick it up the next time you're together. Let's be more specific.

Each of the six sessions in *Growing in Jesus* contains five unique sections. These five sections have the same titles in every book and in every session in the LIFETOGETHER series. The sections are (1) fellowship, (2) discipleship, (3) ministry, (4) evangelism, and (5) worship. These represent five biblical purposes that we believe lead to personal spiritual growth, growth in your student ministry, and health for your entire church. The more you think about these five purposes and try to make them part of your life, the stronger you'll be and the more you'll grow spiritually.

While these five biblical purposes make sense individually, they can make a greater impact when they're brought together. Think of it in sports terms: If you play baseball or softball, you might be an outstanding hitter—but you also need to catch, throw, run, and slide. You need more than one skill to impact your team. In the same way, having a handle on one or two of the five biblical purposes is great—but when they're all reflected together in a person's life, that person is much more biblically balanced and healthy.

You'll find that the material in this book (and in the other LIFETOGETHER books) is built around the Bible. There are a lot of blank spaces and journaling pages where you can write down your thoughts about God's Word and God's work in your life as you explore and live out God's biblical purposes.

Each session begins with a short story that helps introduce the theme. If you have time to read it, great—if not, no big deal. Immediately following the story are five key sections. The following is a brief description of each:

## ♥ FELLOWSHIP: CONNECTING YOUR HEART TO OTHERS'

Goal: To share about your life and listen attentively to others, caring about what they share

You'll begin your session with a few minutes of conversation that will give you all a chance to share from your own lives, get to know each other better, and offer initial thoughts about the session's theme. The icon for this section is a heart because you're opening up your heart so others can connect with you on a deeper level.

## DISCIPLESHIP: GROWING TO BE LIKE JESUS

Goal: To explore God's Word, gain biblical knowledge, and make personal applications

This section will take the most time. You'll explore the Bible and gain some knowledge about Jesus. You'll encounter his life and teachings and discuss how God's Word can make a difference in your own life. The icon for this section is a brain because you're opening your mind to learn God's Word and his ways.

You'll find lots of questions in this section—more than you can discuss during your group time. Your leader will choose the questions you have time to discuss or come up with different questions. We encourage you to respond to the skipped questions on your own; during the week it's a great way to get more Bible study time.

## MINISTRY: SERVING OTHERS IN LOVE

Goal: To recognize and take advantage of opportunities to serve others

When you get to this section, you'll have an opportunity to discuss how to express God's love through serving others. The discussion and opportunities are created to tie into the topic. As you grow spiritually, you'll naturally begin to recognize and take opportunities to serve others. As your heart grows, so will your opportunities to serve. Here, the icon is a foot because feet communicate movement and action—serving and meeting the needs of others requires you to act on what you've learned.

## ✍ EVANGELISM: SHARING YOUR STORY AND GOD'S STORY

Goal: To consider how the truths from this session might be applied to your relationships with unbelievers

It's very easy for a small group to turn into a clique that only looks inward and loses sight of others outside the group. That's not God's plan. God wants you to reach out to people with his message of love and life change. While this is often scary, this section will give you an opportunity to discuss your relationships with non-Christians and consider ways to listen to their stories, share pieces of your story, and reflect the amazing love of God's story. The icon for this section is a mouth because you're opening your mouth to have spiritual conversations with nonbelievers.

## ⟑ WORSHIP: SURRENDERING YOUR LIFE TO HONOR GOD

Goal: To focus on God's presence

Each session ends with a time of prayer. You'll be challenged to slow down and turn your focus toward God's love, his goodness, and his presence in your life. You'll spend time talking to God, listening in silence, reading Scripture, writing, and focusing on God. The key word for this time is *surrender*, which is giving up what you want so God can give you what he wants. The icon for this section is a body, which represents surrendering your entire life to God.

Oh yeah…there are more sections in each session!

In addition to the main material, there are several additional options you can use to help further and deepen your times with God. Many people attend church programs, listen, and then "leave" God until the next week when they return to church. We don't want that to happen to you! So we've provided several more opportunities for you to learn, reflect, and grow on your own.

At the end of every session you'll find three more key headings:

- At Home This Week
- Learn a Little More
- For Deeper Study on Your Own

They're fairly easy to figure out, but here's a brief description of each:

## AT HOME THIS WEEK

There are five options presented at the end of each session that you can do on your own. They're not homework for the next session (unless your leader assigns them to your group); they're things you can do to keep growing at your own pace. You can skip them, you can do all of them, or you can vary the options from session to session.

### Option 1: A Weekly Reflection

At the end of each session you'll find a one-page, quick self-evaluation that helps you reflect on the five key areas of your spiritual life (fellowship, discipleship, ministry, evangelism, and worship). It's simply a guide for you to gauge your spiritual health. The first one is on page 28.

### Option 2: Daily Bible Readings

One of the challenges in deepening your knowledge of God's Word and learning more about Jesus' life is to read the Bible on your own. This option provides a guide to help you read through the Gospel of John in 30 days. On pages 111-112 is a list of Bible passages to help you continue to take God's Word deeper into your life.

### Option 3: Memory Verses

On pages 116-117 you'll find six Bible verses to memorize. Each is related to the theme of a particular session. (Again, these are optional...remember, nothing is mandatory!)

### Option 4: Journaling

You'll find a question or two related to the theme of the session that can serve as a trigger to get you writing. Journaling is a great way to reflect on what you've been learning and evaluate your life. In addition to questions at the end of each session, there's a helpful tool on pages 118-120 that can guide you through the discipline of journaling.

### Option 5: Wrap It Up

As you've already read, each session contains too many questions for one small group meeting. So this section provides opportunities to think through your answers to the questions you skipped and then go back and write them down.

## LEARN A LITTLE MORE

We've provided some insights (or commentary) on some of the passages that you'll study to help you understand the difficult terms, phrases, and people that you'll read about in each Bible passage.

## FOR DEEPER STUDY ON YOUR OWN

One of the best ways to understand the Bible passages and the theme of each session is to dig a little deeper. If deeper study fits your personality style, please use these additional ideas as ways to enhance your learning.

## WHAT YOU NEED TO KNOW ABOUT BEING IN A SMALL GROUP

You probably have enough casual or superficial friendships and don't need to waste your time cultivating more. We all need deep and committed friendships. Here are a few ideas to help you benefit the most from your small group time and build great relationships.

### Prepare to Participate

Interaction is a key to a good small group. Talking too little will make it hard for others to get to know you. Everyone has something to contribute—yes, even you! But participating doesn't mean dominating, so be careful to not monopolize the conversation. Most groups typically have one conversation hog, and if you don't know who it is in your small group, then it might be you. Here's a tip: You don't have to answer every question and comment on every point. Try to find a balance between the two extremes.

### Be Consistent

Healthy relationships take time to grow. Quality time is great, but a great quantity of time is probably better. Commit with your group to show up every week (or whenever your group plans to meet), even when you don't feel like it. With only six sessions per book, if you miss just two meetings you'll have missed a third of what's presented in these pages. When you make a commitment to your small group a high priority, you're sure to build meaningful relationships.

### Practice Honesty and Confidentiality

Strong relationships are only as solid as the trust they are built upon. Although it may be difficult, take a risk and be honest with your answers. God wants you to be known by others! Then respect the risks others are taking and offer them the same love, grace, and forgiveness God does. Make confidentiality a nonnegotiable value for your small group. Nothing kills community like gossip.

### Arrive Ready to Grow

You can always arrive prepared by praying ahead of time. Ask God to give you the courage to be honest and the discipline to respect others.

You aren't required to do any preparation in the book before you arrive (unless you're the leader—see page 84). If your leader chooses to, she may ask you to do the Disciple-

**Doug Fields &
Brett Eastman**

Doug and Brett were
part of the same small
group for several
years. Brett was the
pastor of small groups
at Saddleback Church
where Doug is the
pastor to students.
Brett and a team of
friends wrote DOING
LIFETOGETHER,
a group study for
adults. Everyone
loved it so much that
they asked Doug to
take the same theme
and Bible verses
and revise the other
material for students.
So even though Brett
and Doug both had
a hand in writing
this book, the book
you're using is written
by Doug—and as a
youth pastor, he's
cheering you on in
your small group
experience. For more
information on Doug
and Brett see page
139.

ship (GROWING) section ahead of time so that you'll have more time to discuss the other sections and make better use of your time.

## Congratulations…

…for making a commitment to go through this material with your small group! Life change is within reach when people are united through the same commitment. Your participation in a small group can have a lasting and powerful impact on your life. Our prayer is that the questions and activities in this book help you grow closer to the other group members, and more importantly, to God.

If you're a small group leader, please turn to page 85 for a brief instruction on how best to use this material.

# SMALL GROUP COVENANT

One of the signs of a healthy small group is that all members understand its purpose. We've learned that members of good small groups make a bond, a commitment, or a covenant to one another.

Read through the following covenant as a group. Be sure to discuss your concerns and questions before you begin your first session. Please feel free to modify the covenant based on the needs and concerns of your particular group. Once you agree with the terms and are willing to commit to the covenant (as you've revised it), sign your own book and have the others sign yours.

With a covenant, your entire group will have the same purpose for your time together, allowing you to grow together and go deeper into your study of God's Word. Without a covenant, groups often find themselves meeting simply for the sake of meeting.

If your group decides to add some additional values, write them at the bottom of the covenant page. Your group may also want to create some rules (such as not interrupting when someone else is speaking or sitting up instead of lying down). You can list those at the bottom of the covenant page also.

Reviewing your group's covenant, values, and rules before each meeting can become a significant part of your small group experience.

A covenant is a binding agreement or contract. God made covenants with Noah, Abraham, and David, among others. Jesus is the fulfillment of a new covenant between God and his people.

# SMALL GROUP COVENANT

I, _____, as a member of our small group, acknowledge my need for meaningful relationships with other believers. I agree that this small group community exists to help me deepen my relationships with God, Christians, and other people in my life. I commit to the following:

### Consistency

I will give my best effort to attend each of our group meetings.

### Honesty

I will take risks to share truthfully about the personal issues in my life.

### Confidentiality

I will support the foundation of trust in our small group by not participating in gossip. I will not reveal personal information shared by others during our meetings.

### Respect

I will help create a safe environment for our small group members by listening carefully and not making fun of others.

### Prayer

I commit to pray regularly for the people in our small group.

### Accountability

I will allow the people in my small group to hold me accountable for growing spiritually and living a life that honors God.

**This covenant, signed by all the members in this group, reflects our commitment to one another.**

Date:

Names:

Additional values our small group members agree to

Additional rules our small group members agree to

SESSION 1

# THE COST OF DISCIPLESHIP

 **LEADERS, READ PAGE 84.**

Schoolwork is demanding enough, but when you throw in sports, friends, and a job, life becomes way too crowded. Kyle and Dave could have easily put their spiritual lives aside with all that was going on in their busy lives, but they were committed to their small group and to helping each other grow to be more like Jesus.

For the last year the only time they could meet to talk about being followers of Jesus was early in the morning before school. They met in their school's parking lot once a week at 5:30 a.m. to talk and pray. It wasn't easy. Kyle and Dave could think of a thousand reasons to stay in their beds like everybody else, but they never did—after each get-together, they were grateful they'd made the time. Looking back at the past year, Kyle and Dave are both convinced that they are more faith-filled and confident as followers of Jesus because they made their spiritual partnership a high priority.

Pursuing spiritual growth in your own life is always costly. It's important to understand the cost—as well as the value of what you get in return—when you follow Jesus. In this session we will look at the value of what Jesus offers you, and then you'll have to decide how much you think it's worth.

## ♥ FELLOWSHIP: CONNECTING YOUR HEART TO OTHERS

Goal: To share about your life and listen attentively to others, caring about what they share

Did you know that God loves you just the way you are, and that your spiritual growth won't earn you any more of his love? That's a wild truth! At the same time, God loves you too much to allow you to stay where you are today. He wants you to grow and change. God has a vision for who you can become when you follow Jesus' teachings and live your life filled and powered by God's Spirit.

Just a reminder: There probably isn't enough time in your small-group session to answer every question. Instead choose which ones you'll answer, and then answer the others on your own time. Have fun!

If your group hasn't discussed the small group covenant on page 18, please take some time now to go through it. Make commitments to each other that your group time will reflect those values (and any additional ones you add). One sign of a healthy small group is that it begins each session by reading the covenant together as a constant reminder of what the group has committed to.

1.  Everyone is a bundle of strengths and weaknesses. What's one thing you're pretty good at? Don't be embarrassed—you *are* good at some things!

2.  What are the three most valuable possessions in your life?

## DISCIPLESHIP: GROWING TO BE LIKE JESUS

Goal: To explore God's Word, gain biblical knowledge, and make personal applications

Christians are called to become disciples of Jesus—to follow his ways with their entire lives. While it's easy to read that sentence or hear someone call you a follower of Jesus, it's very difficult to figure out what that really means in your everyday life. I often hear Christians say, "I'm into discipleship" or "I want to disciple others." Great! But what does discipleship look like? This study will explore what Jesus has to say about it.

*Read Matthew 13:44-46.* (If you don't have a Bible, the passage is on page 89.)

1. After reading these two parables, what are your first impressions?

2. If the treasure and the pearl are symbols for salvation, then why did the people in both parables have to sell everything to buy them? Isn't salvation free?

3. In the first parable, the man sold everything in joy. How could he give up everything and still have joy?

4. Do these parables emphasize the power of God changing a life, or do they emphasize our responsibility as Christians? Explain your answer. (If you get stuck, see note on page 27, "Bought.")

5. Based on these parables, is it possible to be a Christian without giving up everything?

6. When you recognize the value of having a relationship with God, how should you respond?

7. How is the message of these parables personal for you this week? Be specific!

*Read Luke 9:23-27.* (If you don't have a Bible, the passage is on page 89.)

8.  According to this passage, what does it mean to "deny" yourself? (Look for specific answers from the text.)

9.  If all Christians are supposed to deny themselves and follow the same thing (Jesus), does that mean we all become the same person, with the same personality, desires, dreams, and so on? Explain your answer.

10. Choose one of the following to answer: What does it mean to...

    *   take up the cross daily?
    *   follow Jesus?
    *   lose your life?

11. Take a moment to get personal: In what specific ways have you denied yourself or lost your life for Jesus? Or are you holding on to something too tightly? Explain.

12. Is there anything in your life that's keeping you from putting Jesus first? What is it?

## MINISTRY: SERVING OTHERS IN LOVE

Goal: To recognize and take advantage of opportunities to serve others

The cost of being Jesus' disciple is high, but Jesus takes the high cost and shows us the benefits (e.g., treasure, pearl). He knows we could never stay on the path toward him unless we knew we'd benefit in some way.

1.  How can others in your group help you stay passionate about following Jesus? What kind of help do you need to remain faithful to God and his ways?

2. Is it a ministry opportunity when you help someone remain faithful to Jesus? Explain your answer.

## EVANGELISM: SHARING YOUR STORY AND GOD'S STORY

Goal: To consider how the truths from this session might be applied to your relationships with unbelievers

When I was a kid I met a professional baseball player at an elementary school assembly. I asked him a bunch of questions about his life, and as he spoke, he made his life appear attractive—and baseball became more attractive to me as well. I decided I wanted to be a baseball player as well.

I often wonder if non-Christians are attracted to Jesus as a result of my life, faith, and how I speak about my role as a follower of Jesus. What about you?

1. Is there anything attractive about being a disciple of Jesus? If so, what are those things and why are they attractive to you?

2. What might a non-Christian find attractive about being friends with a really committed follower of Jesus?

For the health of your small group, be sure to read the clique section on pages 100-101.

It's vital for your group to decide at this first session whether you can invite friends to join your group. Talk about the structure of your group and stick to your decision. If you decide the answer is no, you may be able to invite friends to join you in the next EXPERIENCING CHRIST TOGETHER book—there are six of them, so there's plenty of time! If you're a small-group leader, see the Small Group Leader Checklist on page 84.

# ⚝ WORSHIP: SURRENDERING YOUR LIFE TO HONOR GOD

Goal: To focus on God's presence

You'll find three prayer resources in the appendices in the back of this book. By reading them (and possibly discussing them), you'll find your group prayer time more rewarding.
• Praying in Your Small Group (pages 127-128). Read this article on your own before the next session.
• Prayer Request Guidelines (pages 129-130). Read and discuss these guidelines as a group.
• Prayer Options (pages 131-132). Refer to this list for ideas to add variety to your prayer time.

Spiritual growth can become exciting when you're growing with other friends. As you close this session, imagine the potential highlights of doing life together with friends while following Jesus.

1. What are some potential highlights of doing life together as a group?

2. What is one benefit to you becoming more like Jesus?

3. End this time in prayer. Begin by thanking God for your group and then ask God for strength to pursue being more like him.

## AT HOME THIS WEEK

One of the consistent values of our LIFETOGETHER books is that we want you to have options for growing spiritually on your own during the week. To help with this "on your own" value, we'll give you five options. If you do these, you'll have more to contribute when you return to your small group, and you'll begin to develop spiritual habits that can last your entire life. Here are the five you'll see after every section. (You might try to do one per day on the days after your small group meets.)

### Option 1: A Weekly Reflection

After each session you'll find a quick, one-page self-evaluation that reflects the five areas of your spiritual life found in this book (fellowship, discipleship, ministry, evangelism, and worship). After each evaluation, you decide if there's anything you'll do differently with your life. This page is all for you. It's not intended as a report card that you turn into your small group leader. The first evaluation begins on page 28.

### Option 2: Daily Bible Readings

On pages 111-112 you'll find a list of Bible passages that will help you read through an entire section of the Bible in 30 days. If you choose this option, try to read one of the assigned passages each day. Highlight key verses in your Bible, reflect on them, journal about them, or write down any questions you have from your reading. We want to encourage you to take time to read God's love letter—the Bible. You'll find helpful tips in "How to Study the Bible on Your Own" (pages 113-115).

### Option 3: Memory Verses

Memorizing Bible verses is an important habit to develop as you learn to grow spiritually on your own. "Memory Verses" (pages 116-117) contains six verses for you to memorize—one per session. Memorizing verses (and making them stick for more than a few minutes) isn't easy, but the benefits are undeniable. You'll have God's Word with you wherever you go.

**"I HAVE HIDDEN YOUR WORD IN MY HEART THAT I MIGHT NOT SIN AGAINST YOU." (PSALM 119:11)**

### Option 4: Journaling

You'll find blank pages for journaling beginning on page 121. At the end of each session, you'll find questions to get your thoughts going—but you aren't limited to answering the questions listed. Use these pages to reflect, write a letter to God, note what you're learning, compose prayer, ask questions, draw pictures, record your thoughts, or take notes if your small group is using the EXPERIENCING CHRIST TOGETHER DVD teachings. For some suggestions about journaling, turn to "Journaling: Snapshots of Your Heart" on pages 118-120.

For this session, choose one or more questions to kickstart your journaling.

Of the five options listed here, mark the option(s) that seem most appealing to you. Share with your group the one(s) you plan to do in the upcoming week. This helps you keep one another accountable as you continue to study and grow on your own.

- I'm excited to be in a group because...
- If someone asked me to describe Jesus, I would say...
- Jesus would want me to know...

### Option 5: Wrap It Up

Write out your answers to any questions that you didn't answer during your small group time.

## LEARN A LITTLE MORE

Goal: To help you better understand the Scripture passage you studied in this session by highlighting key words and other important information.

### Parables

The word *parable* comes from two Greek words meaning, "to throw alongside." Parables are simple word pictures, stories, or illustrations "thrown alongside" a spiritual truth. Parables make both the truth and the story difficult to forget. As one of Jesus' favorite teaching methods, parables forced his listeners to move from passive listening to active thinking. When reading a parable (and you'll come across more than 40 in the Gospels), it's important to avoid two pitfalls: 1) ignoring important details, and 2) trying to make every detail mean something.

### Kingdom of Heaven (Matthew 13:44)

This describes a kingdom in which God's way will infuse everything (Matthew 6:10). It will be a kingdom of goodness, joy, and beauty. God withdrew our planet from his kingdom when we humans (whom God had put in charge) rebelled against God's ways. The Bible tells us that God wants to bring us back into his kingdom.

God created the nation of Israel (the Jewish people) as a gathering place of his kingdom, to attract the rest of humanity to join it. As the Old Testament teaches, Israel repeatedly disobeyed God's ways and commands. As a result, God allowed different empires to oppress Israel. By the time of Jesus, the Roman Empire was in charge of Israel. Many Jews were desperate for a leader who would throw out the Romans. The Bible contains many prophesies about a leader called the Messiah (translated as "anointed one"; the Greek word for messiah is *Christ*). Jewish history records several self-proclaimed messiahs, but none brought the kind of change the Jews were looking for.

Jesus was the prophesied Messiah, and God's kingdom was the central message of his teaching. But Jesus had no intention of being a military Messiah to destroy the Romans and establish a political kingdom. Instead he invited everyone to stop pursuing their own agendas and rejoin God's kingdom. God's kingdom was (and is) immediately available to anyone follows Jesus—but only in part. Jesus will ultimately bring his kingdom in its fullness when he returns.

### Bought (Matthew 13:44)

In the parable, the act of buying the field illustrates our responsibility to accept God's free gift of salvation. Jesus knows we don't buy our way into God's kingdom—the kingdom is God's gift to us, which we receive by faith (Romans 4:1-5, Ephesians 2:8-9). Buying the field is Jesus' way of pointing to the cost of cooperating with God and doing things his way rather than our own.

### Take up his cross daily (Luke 9:23)

Roman law declared that prisoners sentenced to die on the cross no longer had any rights as citizens; the state owned them completely. In a similar way, we give up all rights when we come to Jesus as disciples. We now belong to God, who has bought us with Jesus' blood (Romans 6:16-18, 1 Corinthians 6:19-20). We give God the right to decide which of our needs and desires he will meet, and when and how he will meet them. This isn't easy! Abandoning our selfish desires in order to cling to God's design is a constant battle.

*I tell you the truth, some who are standing here will not taste death before they see the kingdom of God (Luke 9:27)*

"It is unlikely that Jesus equated seeing the kingdom of God with experiencing the end of the world. More probably he meant that some of his followers would not die until after they had seen the coming of God's kingdom in his own mission or in the life of the church. The transfiguration was possibly seen as one fulfillment of the saying."[1]

## FOR DEEPER STUDY ON YOUR OWN

1. Check out Luke 14:25-35 for another radical teaching by Jesus about discipleship.

2. Read Romans 8:5-6, 14:17. How much is a kingdom of life, peace, righteousness, and joy worth to you?

3. Read these three passages from Luke 9: verses 18-20, 21-22, and 23-27. Can you see any connection between them? If so, what is it?

## A WEEKLY REFLECTION

Take a minute to reflect on how well you've been doing in the following five areas of your spiritual life this week—a 10 means you did an amazing job. This reflection can serve as a spiritual gauge to help you consider some very important areas. This is for your personal evaluation and growth; it's NOT a test—no one else needs to see it.

[1] Carson, D. A. (1994). *New Bible Commentary: 21st Century Edition*. Rev. ed. of: *The New Bible Commentary*. 3rd ed./edited by D. Guthrie, J. A. Motyer. 1970. (4th ed.) (Luke 9:18). Leicester, England; Downers Grove, Ill., USA: InterVarsity Press.

## FELLOWSHIP: CONNECTING YOUR HEART TO OTHERS

How well did I connect with other Christians?

1  2  3  4  5  6  7  8  9  10

## DISCIPLESHIP: GROWING TO BE LIKE JESUS

How well did I take steps to grow spiritually and deepen my faith on my own?

1  2  3  4  5  6  7  8  9  10

## MINISTRY: SERVING OTHERS IN LOVE

How well did I recognize opportunities to serve others and follow through?

1  2  3  4  5  6  7  8  9  10

## EVANGELISM: SHARING YOUR STORY AND GOD'S STORY

How well did I engage in spiritual conversations with non-Christians?

1  2  3  4  5  6  7  8  9  10

## WORSHIP: SURRENDERING YOUR LIFE TO HONOR GOD

How well did I focus on God's presence and honor him with my life? Was my relationship with God a primary focus?

1  2  3  4  5  6  7  8  9  10

When you finish, celebrate the areas where you feel good and consider how you can use those strengths to help others in their journey to be more like Jesus. You might also want to take time to identify some potential areas for growth.

# IN THE HEAT OF THE DESERT

 **LEADERS, READ PAGE 84.**

Mandy wants to make some big changes in her life. She wants to start living for what she knows is right instead of her own selfish desires. But she's scared that her friends won't understand and will disappear once she begins to get serious about her commitment to Jesus and following his ways.

But after one Sunday morning at church, Mandy finally decided to trust the Holy Spirit's nudging in her life and made her decision. Her radical change left her friends frustrated—they didn't understand why she needed to change. Without her friends, Mandy felt empty walking down the school hallways.

Even though it was tempting, she didn't go back to her friends and their ways. Mandy decided she'd rather be alone and follow God than be with her friends and live selfishly. So Mandy spent a lot of time by herself—journaling, reading her Bible, listening, and praying. She sought guidance from her parents and her small-group leader at church, and they gave her some ideas of how to stay strong and remain faithful in the midst of loneliness and temptation.

One Saturday Mandy went to a homeless shelter with some other students from her church. She enjoyed it so much that she began serving there every week. As a result of her faithfulness, God blessed her with some wonderful new friends—people she had seen at school but had never really taken the time to meet. So not only is Mandy not alone anymore, she's hanging with a much better crowd for her spiritual walk—Christian friends who challenge her to follow God's ways.

Taking risks can feel like heading into the desert. At first you feel empty, dry, lonely, and scared. But if you let God do his work in your life during this alone time, it can be a great season for spiritual growth. In this session we'll look at the difficulty of facing temptation and how hard times can lead to a deeper commitment to Jesus.

## ♥ FELLOWSHIP: CONNECTING YOUR HEART TO OTHERS

Goal: To share about your life and listen attentively to others, caring about what they share

1. When you hear the word desert (not to be confused with a tasty dessert—remember, two s's for two scoops of ice cream!), what images come to mind? Write them down.

2. From among the images you wrote down for question 1, circle the positive ones. Were there any? If not, can you think of any positive images of the desert now?

3. What two temptations are the most difficult for you to resist?

## DISCIPLESHIP: GROWING TO BE LIKE JESUS

Goal: To explore God's Word, gain biblical knowledge, and make personal applications

Before Jesus began his ministry, the Holy Spirit drove him into the desert. This wasn't a resort vacation experience. It was hot, dry, and lonely. While he was there, Jesus experienced significant temptation (Hebrews 4:15). Because of that experience, Jesus is able to relate to the temptations we face. In this session, we're going to see how Jesus handled real temptation from his enemy, Satan.

*Read Luke 4:1-13.* (If you don't have a Bible, the passage is on pages 89-90.)

1. Why do you think Jesus spent 40 days alone in the wilderness?

2. The first verse says that Jesus was led into the desert to be tempted by Satan. Does this mean God wanted him to be tempted? If God knows everything, wouldn't he know that Jesus wouldn't give in to temptation?

3. How did Jesus resist temptation in this passage? Why do you think this method works?

4. What phrase does Jesus repeat in each answer to the devil?

5. What are the three things the devil uses to tempt Jesus? What are some modern comparisons or parallels?

6. Do you agree or disagree with the following statements?

*"Since Jesus' temptations were real, he could have fallen into sin; therefore Jesus couldn't have been fully God."*

*"Since Jesus was God, he couldn't have fallen into sin; therefore it wasn't really temptation."*

Explain your answers.

7. In the third temptation, the devil quotes a promise from Scripture concerning Jesus specifically. Given Jesus' response, does this mean we're not to rely on God's promises? In your opinion, what's the difference between relying on God's promises and putting God to the test?

8. Let's get personal: As a small group, talk about what you can do to help protect each another from your worst temptations (you listed them under Fellowship question 3).

## MINISTRY: SERVING OTHERS IN LOVE

Goal: To recognize and take advantage of opportunities to serve others

We know Jesus didn't have a Bible; and he probably didn't even have pages of Scripture at his immediate disposal. In Jesus' day, the Hebrew Scriptures were copied by hand; they were very expensive...and rolled into huge, heavy scrolls. So the only way he could have taken God's Word into the desert with him was by having Scripture memorized.

1.  What are your opinions about the following statements?

    *Because it's easy to get Bibles today, many of us take God's Word for granted.*

    *Memorizing Bible verses seems impossible.*

    You might consider holding each other accountable to read through the Bible plan on pages 111-112.

2.  Since most people (even Christians) don't read their Bibles on a regular basis, how can you and your group members hold each other accountable to plant God's Word in your hearts? What is the hardest part about memorizing Scripture? Who can help you (and in doing so, serve you) with this?

3.  Is there anything in your life that you can change so you don't bring unwanted temptation to others in your group?

## 👄 EVANGELISM: SHARING YOUR STORY AND GOD'S STORY

Goal: To consider how the truths from this session might be applied to your relationships with unbelievers

Christians are not the only ones who go through desert experiences. Non-Christians also endure long periods that are dry and lonely, times when they're tempted to do wrong. A key difference is that Christians live with a hope that their desert experiences will lead to significant places (like the Promised Land for the Israelites) because they live to honor God.

Do you have a non-Christian friend in the middle of a desert experience? If so, is there anything you're currently doing (or could do) that might bring refreshment to him? You never know how a simple act of kindness during this time might provoke the thought that she needs Jesus in his life.

## 🚶 WORSHIP: SURRENDERING YOUR LIFE TO HONOR GOD

Goal: To focus on God's presence

1. Are you going through a desert experience now—a time in which you feel dry or empty or unusually vulnerable to temptation? If so, share your experience with your group.

2. Pray for anyone who is experiencing a desert situation. Between now and the next time you meet, consider how you might bring refreshment to those in the desert.

## AT HOME THIS WEEK

### Option 1: A Weekly Reflection

Take another self-evaluation that reflects five areas of your spiritual life (fellowship, discipleship, ministry, evangelism, and worship). See pages 40-41.

### Option 2: Daily Bible Readings

Check out the Bible reading plan on pages 111-112.

### Option 3: Memory Verses

Memorize another verse from pages 116-117.

### Option 4: Journaling

Choose one or more of the following options:

- Write down whatever is on your mind.
- Read your journal entry from last week and write a reflection about it.
- Respond to these questions: What role does God's Word play in my life? What is something I learned from my last desert experience? What is my most difficult temptation right now, and how can I look for God in the midst of that temptation?

### Option 5: Wrap It Up

Write out your answers to any questions that you didn't answer during your small group time.

## LEARN A LITTLE MORE

### Forty days (Luke 4:2)

The 40 days Jesus spent in the desert are conceptually connected to the 40 years the Israelites were forced to wander the desert (after God freed them from slavery in Egypt). Israel's desert time tested their faith and obedience, just as Jesus' desert time did. Both Jesus and Israel had to depend on God. Israel frequently failed its tests (just like us). But Jesus always lived in obedience to God. His long experience with solitude wasn't just a test; it was also preparation for the stressful ministry he was about to begin. Without food, he was empty of everything but the presence of the Holy Spirit (Luke 4:1). Desert times teach us to crave the most important thing: God.

### Devil (4:4)

*Devil* literally means "accuser" or "slanderer." In the book of Job, we see the devil accusing Job of false motives and saying that Job was righteous only because God had blessed his life so much. At the beginning of his ministry, Jesus faced the devil's temptations as well. "Satan was an angel put out of heaven because of his rebellion against God, and his desire to assume the prerogatives of divinity seems to be reflected in Luke 10:18."[2]

### Temple (4:9)

In the city of Jerusalem during the time of Jesus, the temple was the central place of worship for the Jews. God commanded the Jews to build the temple as a holy place where offerings were sacrificed, and where God's presence would reside in a special way (see Exodus 25:8). According to the old covenant God made with the Israelites though Moses, the shedding of blood (animal sacrifice) paid for the sins that the people committed (See Leviticus 1-7).

[2]Achtemeier, P. J., Harper & Row, P., & Society of Biblical Literature. (1985). *Harper's Bible Dictionary.* Includes index. (1st ed.). San Francisco: Harper & Row.

*It is written. . .It says... (4:4,8,12)*

The devil tempts Jesus three times, and in response, Jesus quotes from Deuteronomy 6:8 three times. The book of Deuteronomy contains the words of Israel's greatest prophet and leader, Moses, at the end of Israel's 40-year exile in the desert.

*He left him until an opportune time (4:13)*

Satan is like a "roaring lion" (1 Peter 5:8). Even after God leads us out of a time of emptiness, Satan will continue to prowl and stalk us. He'll tempt us to think we got through the last temptation on our own power (that's pride). He will try to get us to use our gifts to serve ourselves. We need to be on guard at all times, fully dependent on God...and the power of his Word.

## FOR DEEPER STUDY ON YOUR OWN

1. Read Ephesians 6:10-18. How does Paul advise you to deal with the devil's temptations?

2. Get more of the context of the Old Testament passages Jesus quoted when he was tempted by reading Deuteronomy 6:4-19; 8:1-5,17-18.

3. The Israelites hated wandering in the desert; they wanted to get to the Promised Land. But later God points out what the desert experience achieved in Deuteronomy 2:7 and Jeremiah 2:2-3. Read those verses. What did it achieve?

4. Read 1 Kings 18-19 and see how Elijah was tempted. Note that the temptation came after a ministry victory. Do you think there's any connection between success and temptation?

5. Read Ephesians 6:17. How is this verse a weapon against temptation?

## A WEEKLY REFLECTION

Take a minute to reflect on how well you've been doing in the following five areas of your spiritual life this week—a 10 means you did an amazing job. This reflection can serve as a spiritual gauge to help you consider some very important areas. This is for your personal evaluation and growth; it's NOT a test—no one else needs to see it.

### FELLOWSHIP: CONNECTING YOUR HEART TO OTHERS

How well did I connect with other Christians?

1   2   3   4   5   6   7   8   9   10

### DISCIPLESHIP: GROWING TO BE LIKE JESUS

How well did I take steps to grow spiritually and deepen my faith on my own?

1   2   3   4   5   6   7   8   9   10

### MINISTRY: SERVING OTHERS IN LOVE

How well did I recognize opportunities to serve others and follow through?

1   2   3   4   5   6   7   8   9   10

### EVANGELISM: SHARING YOUR STORY AND GOD'S STORY

How well did I engage in spiritual conversations with non-Christians?

1   2   3   4   5   6   7   8   9   10

## WORSHIP: SURRENDERING YOUR LIFE TO HONOR GOD

How well did I focus on God's presence and honor him with my life? Was my relationship with God a primary focus?

1    2    3    4    5    6    7    8    9    10

When you finish, celebrate the areas where you feel good and consider how you can use those strengths to help others in their journey to be more like Jesus. You might also want to take time to identify some potential areas for growth.

# PRESSING THE PAUSE BUTTON

 **LEADERS, READ PAGE 84.**

Jake used to lose his temper with his family and friends—even over little things. Frustration simmered inside him all the time. He prayed about it, but his temper still got the best of him—as well as anyone who dared to cross his path.

Something changed in Jake after a friend pointed out just how busy Jake was all the time. He rushed from one place to another, trying to fit in practices, workouts, studying, and a job. He was always in such a hurry that he didn't have time to consider anyone's feelings other than his own. All he could think about was the next thing on the list.

That challenge triggered Jake to make a spiritual-growth decision; he added some daily time with God to his busy schedule. At first, this seemed unproductive. It was difficult for Jake to stay still and listen to God because he was so used to noise and activity. But he kept at it and made this time a priority. Soon Jake clearly saw that not all of the things on his schedule were so important. Eventually he came to terms with his own limits and slowed down the pace of his life. The result? He wasn't angry nearly as much, and he was able to focus on others' needs in a deeper way.

Taking time out for God is one of the most important things we can do for our spiritual growth. In this session, we'll look at the rhythm of Jesus' life and see how it compares to our own.

## ♥ FELLOWSHIP: CONNECTING YOUR HEART TO OTHERS

Goal: To share about your life and listen attentively to others, caring about what they share

1.  Which area of your life seems the busiest?

**HOME  SCHOOL  CHURCH  WORK  SPORTS  MUSIC  FRIENDS  OTHER**

2.  Is it difficult for you to balance activity and quiet time? Explain.

3.  Which phrase comes closest to how you feel about your time alone with God?

    - What alone time?
    - It's okay.
    - Good, but I want more.
    - It's great!
    - I want to be alone with God, but it never seems to make it on my schedule.
    - Other:

## DISCIPLESHIP: GROWING TO BE LIKE JESUS

Goal: To explore God's Word, gain biblical knowledge, and make personal applications

Today our world is filled with so much busyness, pressure, and demands on our time that it's tough to balance school, friends, family, sports, job, fun, homework...you get the picture.

When Jesus walked the earth 2,000 years ago, he also had a full schedule. There were people to teach, sick people to heal, and disciples to hang out with and instruct in God's ways. Yet Jesus kept everything in perspective and in focus because he made time for God the Father.

1.  Read the following passages and describe what was going on when Jesus decided to go off by himself to pray. (If you don't have a Bible, the passages are on pages 90-91.)

    • Mark 1:32-39
    • Luke 5:15-16
    • Mark 6:30-46

2.  Why is it so important to get away from all the noise and be alone? What are your biggest distractions?

3.  Since Jesus was God, and he and the Father were one (John 10:30), why did Jesus need to spend time away from the crowds?

4.  In the third passage (Mark 6:30-46), what is the relationship between Jesus' time with people and his solitude?

5.  What impact does a quiet time have on your day? How does it affect your attitude and actions?

6. When you spend time alone with God, what do you typically do? Where do you go and when? Is there something in your schedule you need to ditch so you can free up more time for God?

7. Think about quiet times for this next week: What's a realistic-yet-challenging goal you can make today? (Be specific!) Have everyone in the group pair up for accountability during the next week and call your partner to see how she is doing with her quiet time goal.

## MINISTRY: SERVING OTHERS IN LOVE

Goal: To recognize and take advantage of opportunities to serve others

1. Based on how you answered the Fellowship question # 2 (page 44), what can the others in your group do to help you carve out some time in your schedule so you can spend more time with God?

2. How could accountability be helpful for you?

3. Respond to this statement:

You can't have a healthy spiritual life without a healthy heart for God…and you can't have a heart for God without spending time with God…and you can't spend time with God without cutting some busyness from your life…

## EVANGELISM: SHARING YOUR STORY AND GOD'S STORY

Goal: To consider how the truths from this session might be applied to your relationships with unbelievers

If you don't have time for your neighbor, it's difficult to do as Jesus commands and love that neighbor (Matthew 22:39).

There are a lot of people so busy living their own lives that they don't have time for others. Busyness can become a hurdle to evangelism.

1. Can you ever be too busy doing the work of God?



2. How might a stressed-out non-Christian respond to this promise of Jesus?

> "COME TO ME, ALL YOU WHO ARE WEARY AND
> BURDENED, AND I WILL GIVE YOU REST."
> (MATTHEW 11:28)



3. What is attractive about a follower of Jesus who is calm, balanced, and has time for important things?



## 👤 WORSHIP: SURRENDERING YOUR LIFE TO HONOR GOD

Goal: To focus on God's presence

1. Take a few minutes of silence and finish this sentence: "God, if I'm going to spend time with you and live a life that brings light to the world (Matthew 5:14), I need to make some changes in my life. Please help me with the following issues…" (You can write your response on page 94.)

2. End your time by praying for each other.

## AT HOME THIS WEEK

### Option 1: A Weekly Reflection

Take another self-evaluation that reflects five areas of your spiritual life (fellowship, discipleship, ministry, evangelism, and worship). See pages 50-57.

### Option 2: Daily Bible Readings

Check out the Bible reading plan on pages 111-112.

### Option 3: Memory Verses

Memorize another verse from pages 116-117.

### Option 4: Journaling

Choose one or more of the following options:

- Write down whatever is on your mind.
- Read your journal entry from last week and write a reflection about it.
- Respond to these questions: Why am I saying "yes" to so many things? What is hurry doing to my spiritual life?

### Option 5: Wrap It Up

Write out your answers to any questions that you didn't answer during your small group time.

## LEARN A LITTLE MORE

*After sunset (Mark 1:32)*

This event occurred on the Sabbath, a weekly day of rest. One of the Sabbath regulations was to avoid carrying objects; this was considered "work." The people of Capernaum brought the sick and demon-possessed to Jesus after sunset because this is when the Sabbath was over. Sunset is the beginning of the new day, from the Jewish point of view—so 9 p.m. Saturday is technically Sunday.

### *The apostles...reported to him (Mark 6:30)*

After the 12 disciples watched him teach and heal for many months, Jesus named them apostles and sent them out in pairs to do what they had seen him do. We don't know how long the disciples were on the road, but when they returned, they reported what happened.

### *Did not even have a chance to eat (Mark 6:31)*

By this time, Jesus was a kind of celebrity and was always surrounded by crowds. While many who came to him were desperate for healing, it's probable that others came to see him in action, to listen to his teaching, and even in the hope that he was the messiah-king who would lead a rebellion against Rome (John 6:14-15).

## FOR DEEPER STUDY ON YOUR OWN

1. Take time out with God this week and read Psalm 1. After you've reflected on its meaning for your life, pray the psalm back to God.

2. In another quiet time, do the same thing with Psalm 84.

3. Read John 7:1-10,14. How did Jesus handle pressure from his family to speed up his ministry and build his fame? What do you learn from this?

## A WEEKLY REFLECTION

Take a minute to reflect on how well you've been doing in the following five areas of your spiritual life this week—a 10 means you did an amazing job. This reflection can serve as a spiritual gauge to help you consider some very important areas. This is for your personal evaluation and growth; it's NOT a test—no one else needs to see it.

### FELLOWSHIP: CONNECTING YOUR HEART TO OTHERS'

How well did I connect with other Christians?

1    2    3    4    5    6    7    8    9    10

### DISCIPLESHIP: GROWING TO BE LIKE JESUS

How well did I take steps to grow spiritually and deepen my faith on my own?

1    2    3    4    5    6    7    8    9    10

### MINISTRY: SERVING OTHERS IN LOVE

How well did I recognize opportunities to serve others and follow through?

1    2    3    4    5    6    7    8    9    10

### EVANGELISM: SHARING YOUR STORY AND GOD'S STORY

How well did I engage in spiritual conversations with non-Christians?

1    2    3    4    5    6    7    8    9    10

### WORSHIP: SURRENDERING YOUR LIFE TO HONOR GOD

How well did I focus on God's presence and honor him with my life? Was my relationship with God a primary focus?

1  2  3  4  5  6  7  8  9  10

When you finish, celebrate the areas where you feel good and consider how you can use those strengths to help others in their journey to be more like Jesus. You might also want to take time to identify some potential areas for growth.

# PERSISTENT PRAYER

 **LEADERS, READ PAGE 84.**

My friend Tim has cancer. Countless people have prayed for his complete healing for more than two years. Friends and family pray for Tim; they pray alone, they pray in church, they pray in small and large groups. Tim has been anointed with oil, and many have laid hands upon him and begged God to free him from cancer. Tim's cancer is unique in that chemotherapy and radiation will not help, and neither will surgery nor transplant. We are not giving up hope for his complete healing, but at this point God has not healed Tim.

Prayer can be confusing and frustrating.

Yet Tim's life is a light to everyone he encounters as he presses on despite the cancer. He speaks hope to others, and God is using Tim's illness in amazing ways to touch many lives.

When you see Tim, you don't see a cancer patient, you see God at work. God is answering our persistent prayers—not in the time or the way we'd prefer—but God is answering faithfully nonetheless. This session is about prayer and learning to pray in the way Jesus taught us.

## ♥ FELLOWSHIP: CONNECTING YOUR HEART TO OTHERS

Goal: To share about your life and listen attentively to others, caring about what they share

As you discuss prayer, be aware that people hold many different opinions about the subject—be careful to respect what others in your group might believe. In one group I was in, someone shared his opinion on prayer and another group member said, "Are you really that stupid?" As you can imagine, the person who had shared never felt safe to do so again. Prayer isn't easy to understand; be prepared to embark on some good discussions about it.

1. Which of the following best describes your attitude toward prayer?

   - I pray all the time and God always answers my prayers.
   - I pray, but I wonder if my prayers ever get to God.
   - I struggle with having a consistent prayer life.
   - I try to talk to God by praying throughout the day.
   - I don't pray...I don't get it.
   - I'm not convinced prayer works.
   - Why pray when God already knows everything?
   - Other:

2. What role did prayer play in your family when you were a child? (For example: We prayed as a family at meal times; I said bedtime prayers; my parents prayed with me; I never prayed; I only heard God's name when someone cussed, etc.)

## DISCIPLESHIP: GROWING TO BE LIKE JESUS

Goal: To explore God's Word, gain biblical knowledge, and make personal applications

The quality of a relationship is directly related to the quality of communication that exists within that relationship. As we saw in our last session, Jesus made it a habit to get away to quiet places to pray and spend time with God. In this session, we're going to look at Jesus' instructions for a healthy prayer life.

*Read Luke 11:1-13.* (If you don't have a Bible, the passage is on pages 91-92.)

1. What does this passage teach about God's character? Read the text carefully for clues.

2. How does what we believe about God affect our prayer lives? Why is our understanding of God important for the effectiveness of prayer?

3. Write down your definition of prayer. Share your definition with the group. pg 121

4. Do these verses suggest that God answers our prayers when we wear him out? Why is persistence or boldness (verse 8) important for prayer? What's the connection?

5. Since God knows everything, why do we have to ask God for anything? Doesn't God already know what we need?

6. In your own words, explain the meaning of each line in Jesus' prayer.

7. What is the purpose of prayer? What does it accomplish in our lives?

8. Why do you think it's sometimes difficult to pray? What are some distractions that you face when praying?

9. Have you ever consistently asked God for something, and God hasn't answered? Why does God sometimes answer "no"?

10. On a scale of 1 (lousy) to 10 (great), how would you rate your prayer life? Explain.

## MINISTRY: SERVING OTHERS IN LOVE

Goal: To recognize and take advantage of opportunities to serve others

Before my turn to speak to a large crowd, I waited backstage and worked on this part of the book you're reading. Then another youth pastor came up behind me and said, "I want to pray for you. Please don't stop working, I just want to lay my hands on your shoulder and pray for you as you work on your message. You look tired, and I know you could use the prayer."

1. How might praying for people minister to them?

2. The youth pastor prayed that God would use what I was writing in big ways. What he didn't know was that I wasn't working on my talk; I was working on this book. Do you think God still answered his prayer? In other words, can you pray for something and instead God answers another concern that you didn't even know about?

##  EVANGELISM: SHARING YOUR STORY AND GOD'S STORY

Goal: To consider how the truths from this session might be applied to your relationships with unbelievers

1. How often do you pray for your non-Christian friends?

2. What do you specifically ask God to do for them? What about for yourself?

3. Is there anything new that someone shared from the answers to the previous question that may change the way you pray for your friends? If so, describe it.

## WORSHIP: SURRENDERING YOUR LIFE TO HONOR GOD

Goal: To focus on God's presence

1. Are there any prayer requests you've shared with your group that you believe God has already answered?

2. Gather into smaller groups of two or three people and have an extended time of prayer. Pray based on how you were challenged by the passage in Luke.

## AT HOME THIS WEEK

### Option 1: A Weekly Reflection

Take another self-evaluation that reflects five areas of your spiritual life (fellowship, discipleship, ministry, evangelism, and worship). See pages 60-61.

### Option 2: Daily Bible Readings

Check out the Bible reading plan on pages 111-112.

### Option 3: Memory Verses

Memorize another verse from pages 116-117.

### Option 4: Journaling

Choose one or more of the following options:

- Write down whatever is on your mind.
- Read your journal entry from last week and write a reflection about it.
- Respond to these questions: Why do I find it difficult to pray? How might I be different if I spent a lot of time talking to God?

### Option 5: Wrap It Up

Write out your answers to any questions that you didn't answer during your small group time.


## LEARN A LITTLE MORE

### Father (Luke 11:2)

Jesus gives us permission to talk to God in a very intimate and approachable way—by calling him "Father." This is extremely rare in the history of world religions. The all-powerful God regards us as family.

### Hallowed (11:2)

To hallow something is to treat it as holy, sacred, and worthy of awe and respect. To pray that God's name is "hallowed" means that we're asking God for him to be known by all as holy, sacred, and worthy of awe and respect.

### Don't bother me (11:7)

Middle Eastern culture was built on honor and shame. Hospitality was a matter of honor, so the host with a visiting friend absolutely had to get food for him—the honor of the host, his family, and the whole village was at stake. The neighbor's boldness (verse 8) was motivated by desperate need. Likewise, a neighbor who asked for help almost always received a positive response. To say no was to shame both the one who asked and the whole community. Jesus' listeners knew this and would have been shocked by the man who told his neighbor to go away. Jesus was saying, "If even this unbelievably rude person eventually responded to bold and persistent requests, how do you think God will respond?"

### Egg...scorpion (11:12)

We don't receive from God just because we ask; we receive from God because he's compassionate, loving, and caring. God isn't angry or stingy. He wants to help us and give us the very best. Some of us have been hurt and disappointed in our lives and wonder why God doesn't seem to be doing anything about it. But we need to be persistent, trusting that God cares and will provide what we need (Philippians 4:19). Even when God allows us to suffer tragedies, we cannot begin to understand, we need to trust that the big picture of his plan for us and those we love will bring good even out of evil.

## FOR DEEPER STUDY ON YOUR OWN

1. Check out James 1:2-8 to see how prayer is connected to surviving difficult times. Prayer isn't just about us talking to God; it's also about listening to God. Read

Ecclesiastes 5:1-7 to get a better idea about the importance of silence in prayer.

2. Read Matthew's account of Jesus' teaching on prayer in Matthew 6:5-15. What additional insights do you find?

3. In 1 Thessalonians 5:17, Paul exhorts us to "pray continually." How do you think a person goes about doing that in a practical way?

4. Read Luke 11:2-13 again. Give each of these sections a title or description based on a type of prayer.

   - 11:2-4
   - 11:5-10
   - 11:11-13

5. Compare the prayer in Luke 11:1-13 to the prayer in Matthew 6:9-13. What do you see that's similar? What's different?

## A WEEKLY REFLECTION

Take a minute to reflect on how well you've been doing in the following five areas of your spiritual life this week—a 10 means you did an amazing job. This reflection can serve as a spiritual gauge to help you consider some very important areas. This is for your personal evaluation and growth; it's NOT a test—no one else needs to see it.

## FELLOWSHIP: CONNECTING YOUR HEART TO OTHERS'

How well did I connect with other Christians?

1    2    3    4    5    6    7    8    9    10

## DISCIPLESHIP: GROWING TO BE LIKE JESUS

How well did I take steps to grow spiritually and deepen my faith on my own?

1    2    3    4    5    6    7    8    9    10

## MINISTRY: SERVING OTHERS IN LOVE

How well did I recognize opportunities to serve others and follow through?

1    2    3    4    5    6    7    8    9    10

## EVANGELISM: SHARING YOUR STORY AND GOD'S STORY

How well did I engage in spiritual conversations with non-Christians?

1    2    3    4    5    6    7    8    9    10

## WORSHIP: SURRENDERING YOUR LIFE TO HONOR GOD

How well did I focus on God's presence and honor him with my life? Was my relationship with God a primary focus?

1    2    3    4    5    6    7    8    9    10

When you finish, celebrate the areas where you feel good and consider how you can use those strengths to help others in their journey to be more like Jesus. You might also want to take time to identify some potential areas for growth.

# BUILDING ON A SOLID FOUNDATION

 **LEADERS, READ PAGE 84.**

Nick wasn't the most popular student, but those who knew him liked him a lot. He was a loyal friend and basically fell into the "good kid" category. He went to church every week, served in a ministry, and was involved in a small group. Nick spent daily time with God, reading the Bible, and praying. He also had a best friend who kept him accountable in his spiritual life, and together they developed some good spiritual habits. God wasn't merely something Nick *did* with his life—God *was* his life.

But life changed suddenly for Nick last spring. His dad suffered a massive heart attack and died. A tremendous tragedy hit Nick's once-unscathed life, and the loss affected everyone in his family. It was a painful time. But Nick knew that God was in control, and that he was a God of hope who would prove himself trustworthy. Nick not only had a loving family to turn to in his pain, but he also had a solid foundation because of the relationship he'd built with God.

In this session you'll learn that while foundations aren't always seen, they're essential for life—especially spiritual life. No question about it: You'll experience at least one major storm in your life, if you haven't already. The question is this: Will it crumble your faith or strengthen it? This session will challenge you to consider life's storms and look at what you're currently using as your life's foundation.

## ♥ FELLOWSHIP: CONNECTING YOUR HEART TO OTHERS

Goal: To share about your life and listen attentively to others, caring about what they share

You don't need to be a construction expert to understand how important a solid foundation is for buildings of all sizes. If the foundation is shaky or unstable, there's no way you'll be able to build on it—or worse yet, if you do, your building will eventually crumble.

1. What word would you use to identify the spiritual foundation of your life?

    - Rock solid
    - Wet cement
    - Almost dry cement
    - Dry cement, but not very deep
    - A sandy foundation
    - What's a foundation?
    - Other:

2. Give a short update about how your life has been going since the last time you met as a group.

## DISCIPLESHIP: GROWING TO BE LIKE JESUS

Goal: To explore God's Word, gain biblical knowledge, and make personal applications

Talk is cheap. You've probably experienced a disappointing situation when someone didn't back up his words with actions. Many Christians know a lot about Jesus and the Bible, but their lives don't reflect it. They can answer all the questions at Bible study and can sound spiritual at any time, but the plain truth is that following Jesus is merely about head knowledge for them. True followers of Jesus love others because that's what Jesus did for all of us. To know Jesus is to put his words into practice in your life.

*Read Luke 6:46-49.* (If you don't have a Bible, the passage is on page 92.)

1. Describe what this parable means to you.

2. How does this parable challenge you personally?

3. The first verse seems to make little sense; why would someone call Jesus Lord but not do what he says? How is this possible?

4. According to this parable, how can we have stability and protection in the midst of life's storms?

5. How are the two house builders different? How are they similar?

6. Since God's Word is true and wise to follow, how is it possible for a person to hear the Word and *not* follow it?

7. In this passage, the floods hit both builders. Are you facing any storms right now? What's happening, and how can your small group help?

8. Since we're saved by faith in Jesus, why is what we put into practice so important? Why can't we just listen to the Word and then do whatever we want?

9. Jesus modeled obedience to the Father. In John 17:4 he says, "I have brought you glory on earth by completing the work you gave me to do." Jesus' disciples knew that obedience was essential to discipleship. Disciples aren't simply learners—they're followers. They obediently follow Jesus and his teachings. What teaching of Jesus do you find particularly difficult to follow?

## MINISTRY: SERVING OTHERS IN LOVE

Goal: To recognize and take advantage of opportunities to serve others

1. Can you explain the connection between obedience to God's Word and meeting needs with love (ministry)? How does obedience become ministry?

2. What would it look like for you to obey what Jesus teaches in the following verses? Pick one and talk about it.

"AND IF ANYONE GIVES EVEN A CUP OF COLD WATER TO ONE OF THESE LITTLE ONES BECAUSE HE IS MY DISCIPLE, I TELL YOU THE TRUTH, HE WILL CERTAINLY NOT LOSE HIS REWARD." (MATTHEW 10:42)

"BUT I TELL YOU, DO NOT RESIST AN EVIL PERSON. IF SOMEONE STRIKES YOU ON THE RIGHT CHEEK, TURN TO HIM THE OTHER ALSO." (MATTHEW 5:39)

**"IF SOMEONE FORCES YOU TO GO ONE MILE, GO WITH HIM TWO MILES." (MATTHEW 5:41)**

3. How does a strong foundation in your life affect your ministry to others? What is something you could do to strengthen your foundation?

## EVANGELISM: SHARING YOUR STORY AND GOD'S STORY

Goal: To consider how the truths from this session might be applied to your relationships with unbelievers

Don't get the wrong idea: Knowledge isn't the most important aspect of your faith, but it's still important—especially when it comes to sharing God's love with others. You need a foundation of knowledge for guiding others to Jesus. Let's continue the building analogy: Before you start construction, you need blueprints that provide directions on where to pour the foundation and where to place the walls—otherwise you might build the wrong house in the wrong lot (or the wrong neighborhood!). It's the same way with evangelism: It's good to know how to say what you want to say *before* you say it!

1. Put the following evangelistic ideas in a progressive order from 1 to 10, with 1 being the action item you do first. (Do this by yourself.)

___ Share your faith story (testimony).
___ Share some key Scriptures about salvation.
___ Listen to the other person's story.
___ Invite the person to church.
___ Ask the person if she knows God.
___ Be her friend.
___ Pray for him.
___ Ask him if he wants to begin a relationship with Jesus.
___ Ask her questions about what she believes.
___ Share some of God's story.

2. Share your 1 to 10 order with your group. Talk about some of the differences you have. This discussion isn't about winning or being right; instead use this discussion as a thoughtful dialog about what's really important when it comes to sharing Christ with others.

## 🚶 WORSHIP: SURRENDERING YOUR LIFE TO HONOR GOD

Goal: To focus on God's presence

1. Is there an area of your life in which Jesus is asking you to obey him? If so, how can the group pray for you?

2. Some students in your group may be facing storms in their lives right now. If so, pray especially for them. It's good for groups to learn how to pray for others in need. The more comfortable you become as a group praying for one another, the more helpful it will be to you individually. At some point, you'll be the one prayed for!

### AT HOME THIS WEEK

#### Option 1: A Weekly Reflection

Take another self-evaluation that reflects five areas of your spiritual life (fellowship, discipleship, ministry, evangelism, and worship). See pages 70-71.

#### Option 2: Daily Bible Readings

Check out the Bible reading plan on pages 111-112.

#### Option 3: Memory Verses

Memorize another verse from pages 116-117.

#### Option 4: Journaling

Choose one or more of the following options:

- Write down whatever is on your mind.
- Read your journal entry from last week and write a reflection about it.
- Respond to these questions: Why is building a foundation difficult? Why would a Christian skip past the foundation-building phase? When a storm hits, I'll…

## Option 5: Wrap It Up

Write out your answers to any questions that you didn't answer during your small group time.

## LEARN A LITTLE MORE

### Hears…puts them into practice (Luke 6:47)

The contrast isn't between hearing and not hearing; it's between doing and not doing. We can hear excellent, Bible-based preaching and have no stronger foundation than someone who never goes to church. Obedience is essential to a firm foundation. If we fail to act on what we believe, then we actually believe nothing and will be washed away when life's storms hit.

### Flood (6:48)

Some storms are worse than others, and devotion to Jesus is no guarantee that you won't suffer a personal hurricane. But consistently hearing and practicing Jesus' words will help you survive the storms and even have something to offer others when storms hit their lives.

## FOR DEEPER STUDY ON YOUR OWN

1. Read Matthew's version of this session's passage (Matthew 7:24-27). What does Matthew emphasize that Luke doesn't?

2. Study Jesus' commands in Luke 6:20-45. Why is each of these commands important as a foundation for life?

3. Read James 2:14-26. How does obedience demonstrate the quality of our faith?

## A WEEKLY REFLECTION

Take a minute to reflect on how well you've been doing in the following five areas of your spiritual life this week—a 10 means you did an amazing job. This reflection can serve as a spiritual gauge to help you consider some very important areas. This is for your personal evaluation and growth; it's NOT a test—no one else needs to see it.

### FELLOWSHIP: CONNECTING YOUR HEART TO OTHERS'

How well did I connect with other Christians?

1    2    3    4    5    6    7    8    9    10

### DISCIPLESHIP: GROWING TO BE LIKE JESUS

How well did I take steps to grow spiritually and deepen my faith on my own?

1    2    3    4    5    6    7    8    9    10

### MINISTRY: SERVING OTHERS IN LOVE

How well did I recognize opportunities to serve others and follow through?

1    2    3    4    5    6    7    8    9    10

### EVANGELISM: SHARING YOUR STORY AND GOD'S STORY

How well did I engage in spiritual conversations with non-Christians?

1     2     3     4     5     6     7     8     9     10

### WORSHIP: SURRENDERING YOUR LIFE TO HONOR GOD

How well did I focus on God's presence and honor him with my life? Was my relationship with God a primary focus?

1     2     3     4     5     6     7     8     9     10

When you finish, celebrate the areas where you feel good and consider how you can use those strengths to help others in their journey to be more like Jesus. You might also want to take time to identify some potential areas for growth.

# WHERE IS YOUR TREASURE?

 **LEADERS, READ PAGE 84.**

Chelsea baby-sits twice a week, and she's very careful with what she earns. She makes sure she has gas money and deposits the rest in her bank account. One of her favorite things is depositing her money and reading the accounting slip to see how fast her cash is piling up. It makes her feel important to know she has money in the bank.

But Chelsea often acts as if she never has any money. She will often say no to activities that require her to spend her own money. In fact, if anyone is ever in financial need, Chelsea is the first to turn away. Recently her small group decided to sponsor a needy child from Haiti (the poorest country in the Western Hemisphere). Chelsea was against the idea; she said she was too young for this kind of responsibility. In truth, she wanted to spend her money her way and not be pressured by others. Even though her small group discussed ways to raise money for this child, Chelsea wouldn't budge. Her small group decided to sponsor the child without her participation.

But after weeks of watching her friends share in the joy of financially helping someone, Chelsea decided that giving her money to someone who needed it was more important than watching it pile up in the bank. Chelsea learned that money is a useful tool but an unreliable master.

In this session, we'll look at what makes you feel most important. Whether you are a big spender or a big saver, we'll talk about what you treasure and why.

## ♥ FELLOWSHIP: CONNECTING YOUR HEART TO OTHERS

Goal: To share about your life and listen attentively to others, caring about what they share

1. If you had a million dollars, what would you do with it?

2. Which of these statements best describes the way you handle money?

   - I don't have any money.
   - Others take care of my financial needs.
   - I don't spend my money; I save it.
   - I have trouble saving money; I usually spend it on stuff for myself.
   - I have trouble saving money; I usually spend it on others.
   - Other:

## DISCIPLESHIP: GROWING TO BE LIKE JESUS

Goal: To explore God's Word, gain biblical knowledge, and make personal applications

Priorities define who we are. It's easy to get tangled up in the chase for bigger, better, faster, and so on. But when we pursue temporary things (such as money), we ultimately end up unsatisfied. We have more things to worry about—and things often become more important to us than they should be. It's easy to get caught up in living life without ever wrestling with priorities and deciding what's really important. In this session, we're going to look at what Jesus had to say about what we treasure.

*Read Matthew 6:19-34.* (If you don't have a Bible, the passage is on page 93.)

1. What are some examples of "treasures on earth" we look for? What two or three earthly treasures do you find yourself regularly pursuing or wanting?

2. According to this passage (read carefully!), what are some differences between earthly treasures and heavenly treasures?

3. Read verses 22-23. What do these verses have to do with what we treasure?

4. Why do you think it's impossible to serve two masters? Is it really impossible, or is it just difficult?

5. Does this passage mean we have to hate money if we love God? Explain.

6. What's the connection between what we treasure and our worries? What are the things you worry about the most? What's the difference between worrying about tomorrow and planning for tomorrow? Now get practical: How is it possible for a person not to worry?

7. Has there been a time when God provided for you in a way you didn't think possible?

8. Read verse 33 again. What do you think it means to seek first God's kingdom?

9. Does verse 33 mean that as long as we focus on God as our top priority that we'll get everything else we want?

10. Is it possible to trust God "too much" and live without any kind of worries or concerns? How do you balance personal responsibility and trusting God?

## MINISTRY: SERVING OTHERS IN LOVE

Goal: To recognize and take advantage of opportunities to serve others

1. You've been together as a group for this entire study, and it's always a good thing to check in with each other and find out if there's anything you can do for others in your group to help them be more like Jesus. Remember: When you're in a group, you're really doing life together—and part of that journey is ministering to each other.

2. When you're hit by temptation to acquire things, build up your savings, and rely on your money, is there anything this group can do to help you keep your priorities straight?

3. Discuss the idea of giving back to God through a weekly tithe. Do you tithe? Do you understand what tith-

ing is, and why Christians must obey God with their money? Does talking about money feel too personal, or is this something that a healthy small group should be able to talk about?

## EVANGELISM: SHARING YOUR STORY AND GOD'S STORY

Goal: To consider how the truths from this session might be applied to your relationships with unbelievers

1. What should be the biggest difference between Christians and non-Christians when it comes to money?

2. Talking to non-Christians about their attitudes about money can be a difficult way to begin talking about Jesus—especially in a time when many non-Christians believe that "the only thing churches want is your money." So, how would you approach a non-Christian who loves money and possessions without sounding like the church is just interested in his wallet?

## WORSHIP: SURRENDERING YOUR LIFE TO HONOR GOD

Goal: To focus on God's presence

1. How has this group helped you grow spiritually? What are you most thankful for? Is there anyone in particular you're proud to call a friend whom you didn't know too well before this group began meeting?

2. In addition to praying for each other, make sure you thank God for the new friendships and the things you learned through this group.

Since this is the last time your group will be together with this particular book as your guide, make sure you take some time to discuss what will happen to your group next. If you want to continue to study the incredible life and teachings of Jesus, there are a total of six books in this series.

## AT HOME THIS WEEK

### Option 1: A Weekly Reflection

Take another self-evaluation that reflects five areas of your spiritual life (fellowship, discipleship, ministry, evangelism, and worship). See pages 80-81.

### Option 2: Daily Bible Readings

Check out the Bible reading plan on pages 111-112.

### Option 3: Memory Verses

Memorize another verse from pages 116-117.

### Option 4: Journaling

Choose one or more of the following options:

- Write down whatever is on your mind.
- Read your journal entry from last week and write a reflection about it.
- Complete these partial statements: When it comes to money, I need... For God to be more important to me than money, I would need to...

### Option 5: Wrap It Up

Write out your answers to any questions that you didn't answer during your small group time.

## LEARN A LITTLE MORE

### Eye is the lamp of the body (6:22)

In ancient Israel, lamps were extremely important. A lamp was the only source of light at night, other than the moon and stars. There were no streetlights, and homes had only one or two lamps each. So whatever a lamp illuminated was what people focused upon. In the same way, the eye is the body's lamp. We focus our eyes on what's important to us because our treasures capture our attention.

Jesus uses this figure of speech to drive home the teaching in verse 21 and then takes it a step further. Earthly treasures are not merely temporary; they also darken everything about us. The pursuit of the temporary only leads to pain and lack of true fulfillment. God has better treasures for us to set our gaze upon; when we focus on what he wants for us, we'll not be left wanting.

### Two masters (6:24)

This general statement becomes more specific at the end of the verse. The two masters are God and money. The idea behind this teaching isn't that we can't follow "two masters" at times—we often have to respect multiple authorities in a wide variety of situations. Instead this passage further explains the second commandment: We cannot worship anything but God because God doesn't want to share our hearts with anything else.

### Loving money

Sometimes I hear Christians say, "Money is the root of all evil." This is a very common misquote of 1 Timothy 6:10. The verse actually reads, "For the love of money is a root of all kinds of evil." Money is not evil in and of itself. It's really just a tool that all human cultures have created. Like any created object, money can take priority in our lives and shut God out. Many people make money their master because they believe it leads to happiness and fulfillment—not true! Just take a look at the lives of many of the rich and famous, and you'll know it's a lie. God deserves to be number-one in our lives; our attitudes toward money are a reflection of our attitudes toward God.

## FOR DEEPER STUDY ON YOUR OWN

1. The Apostle Paul writes that what you build your life with will either be destroyed or last forever (1 Corinthians 3:10-15). What kinds of things do you think will last into eternity?


2. In Luke 18:18-23, Jesus tells a rich man how to get treasure in heaven. What does this man need to do? Why is that an important step for him? How do you think Jesus' instruction to this man applies to you?


3. What other teachings on money do you find in 1 Timothy 6:17-19? Why might this be important for you?


## A WEEKLY REFLECTION

Take a minute to reflect on how well you've been doing in the following five areas of your spiritual life this week—a 10 means you did an amazing job. This reflection can serve as a spiritual gauge to help you consider some very important areas. This is for your personal evaluation and growth; it's NOT a test—no one else needs to see it.

### FELLOWSHIP: CONNECTING YOUR HEART TO OTHERS'

How well did I connect with other Christians?

1    2    3    4    5    6    7    8    9    10


### DISCIPLESHIP: GROWING TO BE LIKE JESUS

How well did I take steps to grow spiritually and deepen my faith on my own?

1    2    3    4    5    6    7    8    9    10

## MINISTRY: SERVING OTHERS IN LOVE

How well did I recognize opportunities to serve others and follow through?

1    2    3    4    5    6    7    8    9    10

## EVANGELISM: SHARING YOUR STORY AND GOD'S STORY

How well did I engage in spiritual conversations with non-Christians?

1    2    3    4    5    6    7    8    9    10

## WORSHIP: SURRENDERING YOUR LIFE TO HONOR GOD

How well did I focus on God's presence and honor him with my life? Was my relationship with God a primary focus?

1    2    3    4    5    6    7    8    9    10

When you finish, celebrate the areas where you feel good and consider how you can use those strengths to help others in their journey to be more like Jesus. You might also want to take time to identify some potential areas for growth.

# APPENDICES

# SMALL GROUP LEADER CHECKLIST

- **Read through "For Small Group Leaders: How to Best Use this Material"** (see pages 85-88). This is very important—familiarizing yourself with it will help you understand content and how to best manage your time.

- **Read through all the questions in the session that you'll be leading.** The questions are a guide for you to help students grow spiritually. Think through which questions are best for your group. Remember, no curriculum author knows your students better than you do! Just a small amount of preparation on your part will help you manage the time you'll have with your group. Based on the amount of time you'll have in your small group, circle the questions you will discuss as a group. Decide what (if anything) you will assign at the end of the session (things like homework, snacks, group project, and so on).

- **Remember that the questions in this book don't always have obvious, neat, tidy answers.** Some are purposely written to cause good discussion without a specific "right" answer. Often questions (and answers) will lead to more questions.

- **Make sure you have enough books for your students and a few extra in case your students invite friends.** (Note: It's vital for your group to decide during the first session whether you can invite friends to join your group. If not, encourage your group to think of friends they can invite if you go through the next EXPERIENCING CHRIST TOGETHER book in this series.)

- **Read the material included in this appendix.** It's filled with information that will benefit your group and your student ministry. This appendix alone is a great reference for students—familiarize yourself with the tools here so you can offer them to students.

- **Submit your leadership and your group to God.** Ask God to provide you with insight into how to lead your group, patience to do so, and courage to speak truth in love when needed.

# FOR SMALL GROUP LEADERS: HOW TO BEST USE THIS MATERIAL

This book was written more as a guidebook than a workbook. In most workbooks, you're supposed to answer every question and fill in all the blanks. In this book, there are lots of questions and plenty of blank space. Explain to your students that this isn't a school workbook—they're not graded on how much they've written.

The number-one rule for this curriculum is that there are no rules apart from the ones you decide to use. Every small group is unique and will figure out its own style and system. (The exception is when the lead youth worker establishes a guideline for all the groups to follow. In that case, respect your leader's guidelines.)

If you need a guide to get you started until you navigate your own way, here's a way to adapt the material for a 60-minute session.

### Introduction (4 minutes)

Begin each session with one student reading the Small Group Covenant (see page 18). This becomes a constant reminder of why you'll be doing what you're doing. Then have another student read the opening paragraphs of the session you'll be discussing. Allow different students to take turns reading these two opening pieces.

### Connecting (10 minutes)

This section can take 45 minutes if you're not careful! You'll need to stay on task to keep this segment short—consider giving students a specific amount of time and holding them to it. It's always better to leave students wanting more time for discussion than to leave them bored.

### Growing (25 minutes)

Read God's Word and work through the questions you think will be best for your group. This section definitely has more questions than you're able to discuss in the allotted time. Before the small group begins, take some time to read through the questions and choose the best ones for your group. You may also want to add questions of your own. If someone forgets a Bible, we've provided the Scripture passages for each session in the appendix.

The questions in this book don't always have obvious, neat, tidy answers. Some are purposely written to cause good discussion without a specific "right" answer. Often questions (and answers) will lead to more questions.

If your small group is biblically mature, this section won't be too difficult. However, if your group struggles with these questions, make sure you sift through them and focus on the few questions that will help drive the message home. Also, you might want to encourage your group to answer the remaining questions on their own.

### Serving and Sharing (10 minutes)

If you're pressed for time, you may choose to skip one of these two sections. If you do need to skip one due to time constraints, group members can finish the section on their own during the week. Don't feel guilty about passing over a section. **One of the strengths of this material is the built-in, intentional repetition in every session. You will have other opportunities to discuss that biblical purpose.** (Again, that's the main reason for spending a few minutes before your group meets to read through all the questions and pick the best ones for your group.)

### Surrendering (10 minutes)

We always want to end the lesson with a focus on God and a specific time of prayer. You'll have several options but feel free to default to your group's comfort level.

### Closing Challenge (1 minute)

Encourage students to pick one option each from the "At Home This Week" section to complete on their own. The more students initiate and develop the habit of spending time with God, the healthier their spiritual journeys will be. We've found that students have plenty of unanswered questions that they will consider on their own time. **Keep in mind that the main goal of this book is building spiritual growth in community—not to get your students to answer every question correctly.** Remember that this is your small group, your time, and the questions will always be there. Use them, ignore them, or assign them for personal study during the week—but don't feel pressure to follow this curriculum exactly or "grade" your group's biblical knowledge.

Finally, remember that questions are a great way to get students connected to one another and God's Word. You don't have to have all the answers.

## Suggestions for Existing Small Groups

If your small group has been meeting for a while, and you've already established comfortable relationships, you can jump right into the material. But make sure you take the following actions, even if you're a well-established group:

- Read through the "Small Group Covenant" on page 18 and make additions or adjustments as necessary.

- Read the "Prayer Request Guidelines" together (pages 129-130). You can maximize the group's time by following them.

- Before each meeting, consider whether you'll assign material to be completed (or at least thought through) before your next meeting.

- Familiarize yourself with all the "At Home This Week" options at the end of each session. They are explained in detail near the end of Session 1 (page 24), and then briefly summarized at the end of the other five sessions.

Although handling business like this can seem cumbersome or unnecessary to an existing group, these foundational steps can save you from headaches later on because you took the time to create an environment conducive to establishing deep relationships.

## Suggestions for New Small Groups

If your group is meeting together for the first time, jumping right into the first session may not be your best option. You may want to meet as a group before you begin going through the book so you can get to know each other better. To prepare for the first gathering, read and follow the "Suggestions for Existing Groups" mentioned previously.

Spend some time getting to know each other with icebreaker questions. Several are listed here. Pick one or two that will work best for your group or use your own. The goal is to break ground so you can plant the seeds of healthy relationships.

1. What's your name, school, grade, and favorite class in school? (Picking your least favorite class is too easy.)

2. Tell the group a brief (basic) history of your family. What's your family life like? How many brothers and sisters do you have? Which family members are you closest to?

3. What's one thing about yourself that you really like?

4. Everyone has little personality quirks—traits that make each one of us unique. What are yours?

5. Why did you choose to be a part of this small group?

6. What do you hope to get out of this small group? How do you expect it to help you?

7. What do you think it will take to make our small group work well?

### Need some teaching help?

Companion DVDs are available for each EXPERIENCING CHRIST TOGETHER book. These DVDs contain teaching segments you can use to supplement each session. Play them before your discussion begins or just prior to the "Discipleship" section in each session. The DVDs aren't required, but they are a great complement and supplement to the small group material. These are available from www.youthspecialties.com.

# SCRIPTURE PASSAGES

## Session 1

### Matthew 13:44-46

44"The kingdom of heaven is like treasure hidden in a field. When a man found it, he hid it again, and then in his joy went and sold all he had and bought that field. 45Again, the kingdom of heaven is like a merchant looking for fine pearls. 46When he found one of great value, he went away and sold everything he had and bought it."

### Luke 9:23-27

23Then he said to them all: "If anyone would come after me, he must deny himself and take up his cross daily and follow me. 24For whoever wants to save his life will lose it, but whoever loses his life for me will save it. 25What good is it for a man to gain the whole world, and yet lose or forfeit his very self? 26If anyone is ashamed of me and my words, the Son of Man will be ashamed of him when he comes in his glory and in the glory of the Father and of the holy angels. 27I tell you the truth, some who are standing here will not taste death before they see the kingdom of God."

## Session 2

### Luke 4:1-13

1Jesus, full of the Holy Spirit, returned from the Jordan and was led by the Spirit in the desert, 2where for forty days he was tempted by the devil. He ate nothing during those days, and at the end of them he was hungry.

3The devil said to him, "If you are the Son of God, tell this stone to become bread."

4Jesus answered, "It is written: 'Man does not live on bread alone.'"

5The devil led him up to a high place and showed him in an instant all the kingdoms of the world. 6And he said to him, "I will give you all their authority and splendor, for it has been given to me, and I can give it to anyone I want to. 7So if you worship me, it will all be yours."

8Jesus answered, "It is written: 'Worship the Lord your God and serve him only.'"

⁹The devil led him to Jerusalem and had him stand on the highest point of the temple. "If you are the Son of God," he said, "throw yourself down from here. ¹⁰For it is written:

"'He will command his angels concerning you

to guard you carefully;

¹¹they will lift you up in their hands,

so that you will not strike your foot against a stone.'"

¹²Jesus answered, "It says: 'Do not put the Lord your God to the test.'"

¹³When the devil had finished all this tempting, he left him until an opportune time.


## Session 3

### Mark 1:32-39

³²That evening after sunset the people brought to Jesus all the sick and demon-possessed. ³³The whole town gathered at the door, ³⁴and Jesus healed many who had various diseases. He also drove out many demons, but he would not let the demons speak because they knew who he was.

³⁵Very early in the morning, while it was still dark, Jesus got up, left the house and went off to a solitary place, where he prayed. ³⁶Simon and his companions went to look for him, ³⁷and when they found him, they exclaimed: "Everyone is looking for you!"

³⁸Jesus replied, "Let us go somewhere else—to the nearby villages—so I can preach there also. That is why I have come." ³⁹So he traveled throughout Galilee, preaching in their synagogues and driving out demons.

### Luke 5:15-16

¹⁵Yet the news about him spread all the more, so that crowds of people came to hear him and to be healed of their sicknesses. ¹⁶But Jesus often withdrew to lonely places and prayed.

### Mark 6:30-46

³⁰The apostles gathered around Jesus and reported to him all they had done and taught. ³¹Then, because so many people were coming and going that they did not even have a chance to eat, he said to them, "Come with me by

yourselves to a quiet place and get some rest."

³²So they went away by themselves in a boat to a solitary place. ³³But many who saw them leaving recognized them and ran on foot from all the towns and got there ahead of them. ³⁴When Jesus landed and saw a large crowd, he had compassion on them, because they were like sheep without a shepherd. So he began teaching them many things.

³⁵By this time it was late in the day, so his disciples came to him. "This is a remote place," they said, "and it's already very late. ³⁶Send the people away so they can go to the surrounding countryside and villages and buy themselves something to eat."

³⁷But he answered, "You give them something to eat."

They said to him, "That would take eight months of a man's wages! Are we to go and spend that much on bread and give it to them to eat?"

³⁸"How many loaves do you have?" he asked. "Go and see."

When they found out, they said, "Five—and two fish."

³⁹Then Jesus directed them to have all the people sit down in groups on the green grass. ⁴⁰So they sat down in groups of hundreds and fifties. ⁴¹Taking the five loaves and the two fish and looking up to heaven, he gave thanks and broke the loaves. Then he gave them to his disciples to set before the people. He also divided the two fish among them all. ⁴²They all ate and were satisfied, ⁴³and the disciples picked up twelve basketfuls of broken pieces of bread and fish. ⁴⁴The number of the men who had eaten was five thousand.

⁴⁵Immediately Jesus made his disciples get into the boat and go on ahead of him to Bethsaida, while he dismissed the crowd. ⁴⁶After leaving them, he went up on a mountainside to pray.

## Session 4

*Luke 11:1-13*

¹One day Jesus was praying in a certain place. When he finished, one of his disciples said to him, "Lord, teach us to pray, just as John taught his disciples."

²He said to them, "When you pray, say:

"'Father,

hallowed be your name,

your kingdom come.

³Give us each day our daily bread.

⁴Forgive us our sins,

for we also forgive everyone who sins against us.

And lead us not into temptation.'"

⁵Then he said to them, "Suppose one of you has a friend, and he goes to him at midnight and says, 'Friend, lend me three loaves of bread, ⁶because a friend of mine on a journey has come to me, and I have nothing to set before him.'

⁷ "Then the one inside answers, 'Don't bother me. The door is already locked, and my children are with me in bed. I can't get up and give you anything.' ⁸I tell you, though he will not get up and give him the bread because he is his friend, yet because of the man's boldness he will get up and give him as much as he needs.

⁹ "So I say to you: Ask and it will be given to you; seek and you will find; knock and the door will be opened to you. ¹⁰For everyone who asks receives; he who seeks finds; and to him who knocks, the door will be opened.

¹¹ "Which of you fathers, if your son asks for a fish, will give him a snake instead? ¹²Or if he asks for an egg, will give him a scorpion? ¹³If you then, though you are evil, know how to give good gifts to your children, how much more will your Father in heaven give the Holy Spirit to those who ask him!"

## Session 5

### Luke 6:46-49

⁴⁶ "Why do you call me, 'Lord, Lord,' and do not do what I say? ⁴⁷I will show you what he is like who comes to me and hears my words and puts them into practice. ⁴⁸He is like a man building a house, who dug down deep and laid the foundation on rock. When a flood came, the torrent struck that house but could not shake it, because it was well built. ⁴⁹But the one who hears my words and does not put them into practice is like a man who built a house on the ground without a foundation. The moment the torrent struck that house, it collapsed and its destruction was complete."

# Session 6

## Matthew 6:19-34

[19] "Do not store up for yourselves treasures on earth, where moth and rust destroy, and where thieves break in and steal. [20]But store up for yourselves treasures in heaven, where moth and rust do not destroy, and where thieves do not break in and steal. [21]For where your treasure is, there your heart will be also.

[22] "The eye is the lamp of the body. If your eyes are good, your whole body will be full of light. [23]But if your eyes are bad, your whole body will be full of darkness. If then the light within you is darkness, how great is that darkness!

[24] "No one can serve two masters. Either he will hate the one and love the other, or he will be devoted to the one and despise the other. You cannot serve both God and Money.

[25] "Therefore I tell you, do not worry about your life, what you will eat or drink; or about your body, what you will wear. Is not life more important than food, and the body more important than clothes? [26]Look at the birds of the air; they do not sow or reap or store away in barns, and yet your heavenly Father feeds them. Are you not much more valuable than they? [27]Who of you by worrying can add a single hour to his life?

[28] "And why do you worry about clothes? See how the lilies of the field grow. They do not labor or spin. [29]Yet I tell you that not even Solomon in all his splendor was dressed like one of these. [30]If that is how God clothes the grass of the field, which is here today and tomorrow is thrown into the fire, will he not much more clothe you, O you of little faith? [31]So do not worry, saying, 'What shall we eat?' or 'What shall we drink?' or 'What shall we wear?' [32]For the pagans run after all these things, and your heavenly Father knows that you need them. [33]But seek first his kingdom and his righteousness, and all these things will be given to you as well. [34]Therefore do not worry about tomorrow, for tomorrow will worry about itself. Each day has enough trouble of its own."

# WORSHIP JOURNAL FOR SESSION 3

"God, if I'm going to spend time with you and live a life that brings light to the world (Matthew 5:14), I need to make some changes in my life. Please help me with the following issues…"

# WHO IS JESUS?

### Jesus is God

The high priest said to him, "I charge you under oath by the living God: Tell us if you are the Christ, the Son of God." "Yes, it is as you say," Jesus replied. (Matthew 26:63-64)

### Jesus became a person

The Word [Jesus] became flesh and made his dwelling among us. (John 1:14)

### Jesus taught with authority

They were amazed at his teaching, for he taught as one who had real authority—quite unlike the teachers of religious law. (Mark 1:22)

### Jesus healed the sick

Jesus went throughout Galilee, teaching in their synagogues, preaching the good news of the kingdom, and healing every disease and sickness among the people. (Matthew 4:23)

### Jesus befriended outcasts

That night Matthew invited Jesus and his disciples to be his dinner guests, along with his fellow tax collectors and many other notorious sinners. The Pharisees were indignant. "Why does your teacher eat with such scum?" they asked his disciples. (Matthew 9:10-11)

### Jesus got angry with religious oppressors

How terrible it will be for you teachers of religious law and you Pharisees. Hypocrites! You are like whitewashed tombs—beautiful on the outside but filled on the inside with dead people's bones and all sorts of impurity. (Matthew 23:27)

### Jesus was persecuted

The chief priests and the whole Sanhedrin were looking for false evidence against Jesus so that they could put him to death. But they did not find any, though many false witnesses came forward. Finally two came forward. (Matthew 26:59-60)

### Jesus was tempted in every way

… for he [Jesus] faced all of the same temptations we do… (Hebrews 4:15)

### Jesus never sinned

… he [Jesus] did not sin. (Hebrews 4:15)

But you know that he [Jesus] appeared so that he might take away our sins. And in him is no sin. (1 John 3:5)

### Jesus died, rose from the dead, and continues to live to this day

But Christ has indeed been raised from the dead… (1 Corinthians 15:20)

### Jesus made it possible to have a relationship with God

For God so loved the world that he gave his one and only Son, that whoever believes in him shall not perish but have eternal life. For God did not send his Son into the world to condemn the world, but to save the world through him. (John 3:16-17)

### Jesus can sympathize with our struggles

This High Priest of ours understands our weaknesses… (Hebrews 4:15)

### Jesus loves us

May you experience the love of Christ, though it is so great you will never fully understand it. (Ephesians 3:19)

### Sound good? Looking for more?

Getting to know Jesus is the best thing you can do with your life. He WON'T let you down. He knows everything about you and LOVES you more than you can imagine!

# A SUMMARY OF THE LIFE OF JESUS

### The Incarnation

Fully divine and fully human, God sent his son, Jesus, to the earth to bring salvation into the world for everyone who believes. *Read John 1:4.*

### John the Baptist

A relative to Jesus, John was sent "to make ready a people prepared for the Lord." He called Israel to repentance and baptized people in the Jordan River. *Read Luke 3:3.*

### The baptism and temptation of Jesus

After John baptized him, Jesus went into the desert for 40 days in preparation for his ministry. He faced Satan and resisted the temptation he offered by quoting Scripture. *Read Matthew 4:4.*

### Jesus begins his ministry

The world's most influential person taught with authority, healed with compassion, and inspired with miracles. *Read Luke 4:15.*

### Jesus' model of discipleship

Jesus called everyone to follow him—without reservation—and to love God and others. *Read Luke 9:23, 57-62.*

### The opposition

The religious "upper class" opposed Jesus, seeking to discredit him in the eyes of the people. Jesus criticized their hypocrisy and love of recognition. *Read Matthew 23:25.*

### The great "I Am"

Jesus claimed to be the bread of life; the light of the world; the good shepherd; and the way, the truth, and the life. Each of these titles reveals essential truth about who he is. *Read John 14:6.*

### The great physician

His words brought conviction and comfort; his actions shouted to the world his true nature. Healing the sick, Jesus demonstrated his power and authority by helping people where they needed it most so they might accept the truth. *Read Matthew 14:14.*

### The great forgiver

Humanity's deepest need is forgiveness and freedom from the guilt of the past—which separates us from God. Only God has the power to forgive, and Jesus further demonstrated his divinity by forgiving the guilty. *Read Matthew 9:6.*

### The disciples

Jesus chose 12 ordinary men to change the world. They weren't rich, powerful, or influential. They had shady pasts, often made huge mistakes, and were filled with doubts. In spite of these things, Jesus used them to build his church. *Read Mark 3:14.*

### The final night

On the night before his death, Jesus spent the time preparing his disciples, and he spent time alone. Obedient to the Father, Jesus was committed to go to the cross to pay the penalty for our sins. *Read Mark 14:32 ff.*

### The Crucifixion

Jesus died a real death on the cross for the sins of the world. His ultimate sacrifice is something all believers should remember often. *Read John 19:30.*

### The Resurrection

After dying on the cross, Jesus was raised from the dead by God's power. This miracle has never been disproved and validates everything Jesus taught. *Read 1 Corinthians 15:55.*

Want a more detailed chronology of Jesus' life and ministry on earth? Check out these two Web sites:

http://www.bookofjesus.com/bojchron.htm

http://mb-soft.com/believe/txh/gospgosp.htm

# SMALL GROUP ROSTER

| NAME | E-MAIL | PHONE | ADDRESS / CITY / ZIP CODE | SCHOOL/GRADE |
|------|--------|-------|---------------------------|--------------|
|      |        |       |                           |              |
|      |        |       |                           |              |
|      |        |       |                           |              |
|      |        |       |                           |              |
|      |        |       |                           |              |
|      |        |       |                           |              |
|      |        |       |                           |              |
|      |        |       |                           |              |
|      |        |       |                           |              |
|      |        |       |                           |              |

# HOW TO KEEP YOUR GROUP FROM BECOMING A CLIQUE

We all want to belong—God created us to be connected in community with one another. But the same drive that creates healthy community can also create negative community, often called a clique. A clique isn't just a group of friends—it's a group of friends uninterested in anyone outside their group. Cliques result in pain for those who are excluded.

If you read the second paragraph of the introduction (page 7), you see the words *spiritual community* used to describe your small group. If your small group becomes a clique, it's an unspiritual community. You have a clique when the biblical purpose of fellowship turns inward. That's ugly. It's the opposite of what God intended the body of Christ to be. Here's why:

- Cliques make your youth ministry look bad.

- Cliques make your small group appear immature.

- Cliques hurt the feelings of excluded people.

- Cliques contradict the value God places on each person.

- Few things are as unappealing as a youth ministry filled with cliques.

Many leaders avoid using their small groups as a way toward spiritual growth because they fear their groups will become cliques. But when they're healthy, small groups can improve your youth ministry's well-being, friendliness, and depth. The apostle Paul reminds us, "Be wise in the way you act toward outsiders; make the most of every opportunity" (Colossians 4:5).

Here are some ideas for being wise and preventing your small group from turning into a clique:

## Be Aware

Learn to recognize when outsiders are uncomfortable with your group. It's easy to forget when you're an insider how bad it feels to be an outsider.

## Reach Out

Once you're aware of someone feeling left out, make efforts to be friendly. Smile, shake hands, say hello, ask him or her to sit with you or your group, and ask simple yet personal questions. An outsider may come across as defensive, so be as accepting as possible.

## Launch New Small Groups

Any small group with the attitude of "us four and no more" has become a clique. A time will come when your small group should launch into multiple small groups if it gets too big—because the bigger a small group gets, the less healthy it becomes. If your small group understands this, you can foster a culture of growth and fellowship.

## For Students Only

Small group members expect adult leaders to confront them for acting like a clique. But instead of waiting for an adult to make the move, shock everyone by stepping up and challenging what you know is destructive. Take a risk. Be a spokesperson for your youth ministry and your student peers by leading the way. Be part of a small group that isn't cliquey and don't be afraid to challenge those who are.

# SPIRITUAL HEALTH ASSESSMENT

Evaluating your spiritual journey is important—that's why we've encouraged you to take a brief survey at the end of each session. The following few pages are simply longer versions of that short evaluation tool.

Your spiritual journey will take you to low spots as well as high places. Spiritual growth is not a smooth incline—a loopy roller coaster is more like it. When you regularly consider your life, you'll develop an awareness of God's Spirit working in you. Evaluate. Think. Learn. Grow.

The assessment in this section is a tool, not a test. The purpose of this tool is to help you evaluate where you are in your faith journey. No one is perfect, so don't worry about your score. It won't be published in your church bulletin. Be honest so you have an accurate idea of how you're doing.

When you finish, celebrate the areas where you're relatively healthy and think about how you can use your strengths to help others on their spiritual journeys. Then think of ways your group members can help one another to improve weak areas through support and example.

## FELLOWSHIP: CONNECTING YOUR HEART TO OTHERS

1. I meet consistently with a small group of Christians.

| 1 | 2 | 3 | 4 | 5 |
|---|---|---|---|---|
| POOR | | | | OUTSTANDING |

2. I'm connected to other Christians who hold me accountable.

| 1 | 2 | 3 | 4 | 5 |
|---|---|---|---|---|
| POOR | | | | OUTSTANDING |

3. I can talk with my small group leader when I need help, advice, or support.

| 1 | 2 | 3 | 4 | 5 |
|---|---|---|---|---|
| POOR | | | | OUTSTANDING |

4. My Christian friends are a significant source of strength and stability in my life.

| 1 | 2 | 3 | 4 | 5 |
|---|---|---|---|---|
| POOR | | | | OUTSTANDING |

5. I regularly pray for others in my small group outside of our meetings.

| 1 | 2 | 3 | 4 | 5 |
|---|---|---|---|---|
| POOR | | | | OUTSTANDING |

6. I have resolved all conflicts with other people—both Christians and non-Christians.

| 1 | 2 | 3 | 4 | 5 |
|---|---|---|---|---|
| POOR | | | | OUTSTANDING |

7. I've done all I possibly can to be a good son or daughter and brother or sister.

| 1 | 2 | 3 | 4 | 5 |
|---|---|---|---|---|
| POOR | | | | OUTSTANDING |

TOTAL:_____

Take time to answer the following questions to further evaluate your spiritual health. You can do this after your small group meets if you don't have time during the meeting. If you need help with this, schedule a time with your small group leader to talk about your spiritual health.

8. List the three most significant relationships you have right now. Why are these people important to you?

9. How would you describe the benefit from being in fellowship with other Christians?

10. Do you have an accountability partner? If so, what have you been doing to hold each other accountable? If not, how can you get one?

## DISCIPLESHIP: GROWING TO BE LIKE JESUS

11. I have regular times of conversation with God.

| 1 | 2 | 3 | 4 | 5 |
|---|---|---|---|---|
| POOR | | | | OUTSTANDING |

12. I'm closer to God this month than I was last month.

| 1 | 2 | 3 | 4 | 5 |
|---|---|---|---|---|
| POOR | | | | OUTSTANDING |

13. I'm making better decisions this month compared to last month.

| 1 | 2 | 3 | 4 | 5 |
|---|---|---|---|---|
| POOR | | | | OUTSTANDING |

14. I regularly attend church services and grow spiritually as a result.

| 1 | 2 | 3 | 4 | 5 |
|---|---|---|---|---|
| POOR | | | | OUTSTANDING |

15. I consistently honor God with my finances through giving.

| 1 | 2 | 3 | 4 | 5 |
|---|---|---|---|---|
| POOR | | | | OUTSTANDING |

16. I regularly study the Bible on my own.

| 1 | 2 | 3 | 4 | 5 |
|---|---|---|---|---|
| POOR | | | | OUTSTANDING |

17. I regularly memorize Bible verses or passages.

| 1 | 2 | 3 | 4 | 5 |
|---|---|---|---|---|
| POOR | | | | OUTSTANDING |

TOTAL:_____

Take time to answer the following questions to further evaluate your spiritual health. You can do this after your small group meets if you don't have time during the meeting. If you need help with this, schedule a time with your small group leader to talk about your spiritual health.

18. What books or chapters from the Bible have you read during the last month?

19. What has God been teaching you lately from Scripture?

20. What was the last verse you memorized? When did you memorize it? Describe the last time a memorized Bible verse helped you.

## MINISTRY: SERVING OTHERS IN LOVE

21. I am currently serving in some ministry capacity.

| 1 | 2 | 3 | 4 | 5 |
|---|---|---|---|---|
| POOR | | | | OUTSTANDING |

22. I'm effectively ministering where I'm serving.

| 1 | 2 | 3 | 4 | 5 |
|---|---|---|---|---|
| POOR | | | | OUTSTANDING |

23. Generally I have a humble attitude when I serve others.

| 1 | 2 | 3 | 4 | 5 |
|---|---|---|---|---|
| POOR | | | | OUTSTANDING |

24. I understand God has created me as a unique individual, and he has a special plan for my life.

| 1 | 2 | 3 | 4 | 5 |
|---|---|---|---|---|
| POOR | | | | OUTSTANDING |

25. When I help others, I typically don't look for anything in return.

| 1 | 2 | 3 | 4 | 5 |
|---|---|---|---|---|
| POOR | | | | OUTSTANDING |

26. My family and friends consider me generally unselfish.

| 1 | 2 | 3 | 4 | 5 |
|---|---|---|---|---|
| POOR | | | | OUTSTANDING |

27. I'm usually sensitive to others' hurts and respond in a caring way.

| 1 | 2 | 3 | 4 | 5 |
|---|---|---|---|---|
| POOR | | | | OUTSTANDING |

TOTAL:_____

Take time to answer the following questions to further evaluate your spiritual health. You can do this after your small group meets if you don't have time during the meeting. If you need help with this, schedule a time with your small group leader to talk about your spiritual health.

28. If you're currently serving in a ministry, why are you serving? If not, what's kept you from getting involved?

29. What spiritual lessons have you learned while serving?

30. What frustrations have you experienced as a result of serving?

## EVANGELISM: SHARING YOUR STORY AND GOD'S STORY

31. I regularly pray for my non-Christian friends.

| 1 | 2 | 3 | 4 | 5 |
|---|---|---|---|---|
| POOR | | | | OUTSTANDING |

32. I invite my non-Christian friends to church.

| 1 | 2 | 3 | 4 | 5 |
|---|---|---|---|---|
| POOR | | | | OUTSTANDING |

33. I talk about my faith with others.

| 1 | 2 | 3 | 4 | 5 |
|---|---|---|---|---|
| POOR | | | | OUTSTANDING |

34. I pray for opportunities to share what Jesus has done in my life.

| 1 | 2 | 3 | 4 | 5 |
|---|---|---|---|---|
| POOR | | | | OUTSTANDING |

35. People know I'm a Christian because of what I do, not just because of what I say.

| 1 | 2 | 3 | 4 | 5 |
|---|---|---|---|---|
| POOR | | | | OUTSTANDING |

36. I feel strong compassion for non-Christians.

| 1 | 2 | 3 | 4 | 5 |
|---|---|---|---|---|
| POOR | | | | OUTSTANDING |

37. I have written my testimony and am ready to share it.

| 1 | 2 | 3 | 4 | 5 |
|---|---|---|---|---|
| POOR | | | | OUTSTANDING |

TOTAL:_____

Take time to answer the following questions to further evaluate your spiritual health. You can do this after your small group meets if you don't have time during the meeting. If you need help with this, schedule a time with your small group leader to talk about your spiritual health.

38. Describe any significant spiritual conversations you've had with non-Christians during the last month.

39. Have non-Christians ever challenged your faith? If yes, describe how.

40. Describe some difficulties you've faced when sharing your faith.

41. What successes have you experienced recently in personal evangelism? (Success isn't limited to bringing people to salvation directly. Helping someone take a step closer at any point on his or her spiritual journey is success.)

## WORSHIP: SURRENDERING YOUR LIFE TO HONOR GOD

42. I consistently participate in Sunday and midweek worship experiences at church.

| 1 | 2 | 3 | 4 | 5 |
|---|---|---|---|---|
| POOR | | | | OUTSTANDING |

43. My heart breaks over the things that break God's heart.

| 1 | 2 | 3 | 4 | 5 |
|---|---|---|---|---|
| POOR | | | | OUTSTANDING |

44. I regularly give thanks to God.

| 1 | 2 | 3 | 4 | 5 |
|---|---|---|---|---|
| POOR | | | | OUTSTANDING |

45. I'm living a life that, overall, honors God.

| 1 | 2 | 3 | 4 | 5 |
|---|---|---|---|---|
| POOR | | | | OUTSTANDING |

46. I have an attitude of wonder and awe toward God.

| 1 | 2 | 3 | 4 | 5 |
|---|---|---|---|---|
| POOR | | | | OUTSTANDING |

47. I often use the free access I have into God's presence.

1          2          3          4          5

POOR                                OUTSTANDING

TOTAL:_____

Take time to answer the following questions to further evaluate your spiritual health. You can do this after your small group meets if you don't have time during the meeting. If you need help with this, schedule a time with your small group leader to talk about your spiritual health.

48. Make a list of your top five priorities. You can get a good idea of your priorities by evaluating how you spend your time. Be realistic and honest. Are your priorities are in the right order? Do you need to get rid of some or add new priorities? (As a student you may have some limitations. This isn't ammo for dropping out of school or disobeying parents!)

49. List 10 things you're thankful for.

50. What influences, directs, guides, or controls you the most?

# DAILY BIBLE READINGS

As you meet with your small group for Bible study, prayer, and encouragement, you'll grow spiritually. But no matter how wonderful your small group experience, you need to learn to grow spiritually on your own, too. God has given you an incredible tool to help—his love letter, the Bible. The Bible reveals God's love for you and gives directions for living life to the fullest.

To help you with this, we've included a fairly easy way to read through one of the Gospels. Instead of feeling like you need to sit down and read the entire book at once, we've broken down the reading into bite-size chunks. Check off the passages as you read them. Don't feel guilty if you miss a daily reading. Simply do your best to develop the habit of being in God's Word daily.

## A 30-Day Journey Through the Gospel of John

Imagine sitting at the feet of Jesus himself: the Teacher who knows how to live life well, the Savior who died for you, the Lord who commands the universe. Like his first disciples, you can follow him around, watch what he does, listen to what he says, and pattern your life after his.

| Day 1 | John 1:1–18 |
| Day 2 | John 1:19–51 |
| Day 3 | John 2:1–11 |
| Day 4 | John 2:12–25 |
| Day 5 | John 3:1–21 |
| Day 6 | John 3:22–36 |
| Day 7 | John 4 |
| Day 8 | John 5:1–15 |
| Day 9 | John 5:16–47 |
| Day 10 | John 6:1–24 |
| Day 11 | John 6:25–71 |
| Day 12 | John 7:1–24 |
| Day 13 | John 7:25–53 |

# HOW TO STUDY THE BIBLE ON YOUR OWN

The Bible is the foundation for all the books in the EXPERIENCING CHRIST TOGETHER series. Every lesson contains a Bible passage for your small group to study and apply. To maximize the impact of your small group experience, it's helpful if each participant spends time reading and studying the Bible during the week. When you read the Bible for yourself, you can have discussions based on what *you* know the Bible says instead of what another member has heard second- or third-hand about the Bible.

Growing Christians learn to study the Bible so they can grow spiritually on their own. Here are some principles about studying the Bible to help you give God's Word a central place in your life.

## Choose a Time and Place

Since we are easily distracted, pick a time when you're at your best. If you're a morning person, then study the Bible in the morning. Find a place away from phones, computers, and TVs so you are less likely to be interrupted.

## Begin with Prayer

Acknowledge God's presence with you. Thank him for his gifts, confess your sins, and ask for his guidance and understanding as you study his love letter to you.

## Start with Excitement

We often take God's Word for granted and forget what an incredible gift we have. God wasn't forced to reach out to us, but he did. He's made it possible for us to know him, understand his directions, and be encouraged—all through his Word, the Bible. Remind yourself how amazing it is that God wants you to know him.

## Read the Passage

After choosing a passage, read it several times. You might want to read it slowly, pausing after each sentence. If possible, read it out loud. (Remember that before the Bible was written on paper, it was spoken verbally from generation to generation.)

## Keep a Journal

Respond to God's Word by writing down how you're challenged, truths to remember, thanksgiving and praise, sins to confess, commands to obey, or any other thoughts you have.

### Dig Deep

When you read the Bible, look deeper than the plain meaning of the words. Here are a few ideas about what to look for:

- *Truth about God's character.* What do the verses reveal about God's character?

- *Truth about your life and our world.* You don't have to figure out life on your own. Life can be difficult, but when you know how the world works, you can make good decisions guided by wisdom from God.

- *Truth about the world's past.* The Bible reveals God's intervention in our mistakes and triumphs throughout history. The choices we read about—good and bad—serve as examples to challenge us to greater faith and obedience. (See Hebrews 11:1-12:1.)

- *Truth about our actions.* God will never leave you stranded. Although he allows us all to go through hard times, he is always with us. Our actions have consequences and rewards. Just like he does in Bible stories, God can use all of the consequences and rewards caused by our actions to help others.

As you read, ask these four questions to help you learn from the Bible:

- What do these verses teach me about who God is, how he acts, and how people respond?

- What does this passage teach about the nature of the world?

- What wisdom can I learn from what I read?

- How should I change my life because of what I learned from these verses?

### Ask Questions

You may be tempted to skip over parts you don't understand, but don't give up too easily. Understanding the Bible can be hard work. If you come across a word you don't know, look it up in a regular dictionary or a Bible dictionary. If you come across a verse that seems to contradict another verse, see whether your Bible has any notes to explain it. Write down your questions and ask someone who has more knowledge about the Bible than you. Buy or borrow a study Bible or check the Internet. Try *www.gotquestions.org* or *www.carm.org* for answers to your questions.

## Apply the Truth to Your Life

The Bible should make a difference in your life. It contains the help you need to live the life God intended. Knowledge of the Bible without personal obedience is worthless and causes hypocrisy and pride. Take time to consider the condition of your thinking, attitudes, and actions, and wonder about how God is working in you. Think about your life situation and how you can serve others better.

## More Helpful Ideas

- Decide that the time you have set aside for Bible reading and study is nonnegotiable. Don't let other activities squeeze Bible study time out of your schedule.

- Avoid the extremes of being ritualistic (reading a chapter just to mark it off a list) and being lazy (giving up).

- Begin with realistic goals and boundaries for your study time. If five to seven minutes a day proves a challenge at the beginning, make it a goal to start smaller and increase your time slowly. Don't set yourself up to fail.

- Be open to the leading and teaching of God's Spirit.

- Love God like he's the best friend you'll ever have—which is the truth!

# MEMORY VERSES

The word *memory* may cause some of you to groan. In school, you have to memorize dates, places, times, and outcomes. Now you have to memorize the Bible?

No, not the entire Bible! Start small with some key verses. Trust us, this is important. Here's why: Scripture memorization is a good habit for a growing Christian to develop because when God's Word is planted in your mind and heart, it has a way of influencing how you live. King David understood this: "I have hidden your word in my heart that I might not sin against you" (Psalm 119:11).

Challenge one another in your small group to memorize the six verses below—one for each time your small group meets. Hold each other accountable by asking about one another's progress. Write the verses on index cards and keep them handy so you can learn and review them when you have a free moment (standing in line, before class starts, sitting at a red light, when you've finished a test and others are still working, waiting for your dad to get out of the bathroom—you get the picture). You'll be surprised at how many verses you can memorize as you work toward this goal and add verses to your list.

"LOVE THE LORD YOUR GOD WITH ALL YOUR HEART AND WITH ALL YOUR SOUL AND WITH ALL YOUR STRENGTH." —DEUTERONOMY 6:5

"PRIDE ONLY BREEDS QUARRELS, BUT WISDOM IS FOUND IN THOSE WHO TAKE ADVICE." —PROVERBS 13:10

"SEE, HE IS PUFFED UP; HIS DESIRES ARE NOT UPRIGHT BUT THE RIGHTEOUS WILL LIVE BY HIS FAITH." —HABAKKUK 2:4

"BUT SOLID FOOD IS FOR THE MATURE, WHO BY CONSTANT USE HAVE TRAINED THEMSELVES TO DISTINGUISH GOOD FROM EVIL."
—HEBREWS 5:14

"LET US FIX OUR EYES ON JESUS, THE AUTHOR AND PERFECTER OF OUR FAITH, WHO FOR THE JOY SET BEFORE HIM ENDURED THE CROSS, SCORNING ITS SHAME, AND SAT DOWN AT THE RIGHT HAND OF THE THRONE OF GOD." —HEBREWS 12:2

"LOVE MEANS DOING WHAT GOD HAS COMMANDED US, AND HE HAS COMMANDED US TO LOVE ONE ANOTHER, JUST AS YOU HEARD FROM THE BEGINNING." —2 JOHN 1:6 NLT

# JOURNALING: SNAPSHOTS OF YOUR HEART

In the simplest terms, journaling is reflection with pen in hand. A growing life needs time to reflect, so several times throughout this book you're asked to journal. In addition, you always have a journaling option at the end of each session. Through these writing opportunities, you're getting a taste of what it means to journal.

When you take time to write your thoughts in a journal, you'll experience many benefits. A journal is more than a diary—it's a series of snapshots of your heart. The goal of journaling is to slow down your life to capture some of the great, crazy, wonderful, chaotic, painful, encouraging, angering, confusing, joyful, and loving thoughts, feelings, and ideas in your life. Keeping a journal can become a powerful habit when you reflect on your life and how God is working in it.

## Personal Insights

When confusion abounds in your life, disorderly thoughts and feelings often loom just out of range, slightly out of focus. Putting these thoughts and feelings on paper is like corralling and domesticating wild beasts. Once on paper, you can look at them, consider them, contemplate the reasons they were causing you pain, and learn from them.

Have you ever had trouble answering the question, "How do you feel?" Journaling compels you to become more specific with your generalized thoughts and feelings. This is not to suggest that a page full of words perfectly represents what's happening on the inside. That would be foolish. But journaling can move you closer to understanding more about yourself.

## Reflection and Examination

With journaling, you can write about your feelings, your situations, how you responded to events. You can reflect and answer questions like these:

- Was that the right response?

- What were my other options?

- Did I lose control and act impulsively?

- If this happened again, should I do the same thing? Would I do the same thing?

- How can I be different as a result of this situation?

## Spiritual Insights

One of the main goals of journaling is to gain new spiritual insights about God, yourself, and the world. When you take time to journal, you have the opportunity to pause and consider how God is working in your life and in the lives of those around you. Journaling helps you see the work he's accomplishing and remember it for the future.

## What to Write About

There isn't one right way to journal, no set number of times per week, no rules for the length of each journal entry. Figure out what works best for you. Get started with these options:

### Write a letter or prayer to God

Many Christians struggle with maintaining a consistent prayer life. Writing out your prayers can help strengthen it. Begin with this question: "What do I want to tell God right now?"

### Write a letter or conversation to another person

Sometimes conversations with others can be difficult because we're not sure what we ought to say. Have you ever walked away from an interaction and 20 minutes later thought, *I should have said...*? Journaling conversations before they happen can help you think through the issues and approach your interactions with others in intentional ways. As a result, you can feel confident as you begin your conversations because you've taken time to consider the issues beforehand.

### Process conflict and pain

You may find it helpful to write about your conflicts with others, especially those that take you by surprise. By journaling soon after conflict occurs, you can reflect and learn from it. You'll be better prepared for the next time you face a similar situation. Conflicts are generally difficult to navigate. Thinking through and writing about specific conflicts typically yields helpful personal insights.

When you're experiencing pain is also a good time to settle your thoughts and consider the nature of your feelings. The great thing about exploring your feelings is that you're only accountable to God. You don't have to worry about hurting anyone's feelings by what you write in your journal (if you keep it private).

### Examine your motives

The Bible is clear regarding two heart truths. First, how you behave reflects who you are on the inside (Luke 6:45). Second, you can take the right action for the wrong reason (James 4:3).

The condition of your heart is vitally important. Molding your motives to God's desires is central to following Christ. The Pharisees did many of the right things, but for the wrong reasons. Reflect on the *real* reasons why you do what you do.

### Anticipate your actions

Have you ever gone to bed thinking, *That was a mistake. I didn't intend that to happen!* Probably! No one is perfect. You can't predict all of the consequences of your actions. But reflecting on how your actions could affect others will guide you and help you relate better to others.

### Reflect on God's work in your life

If you journal in the evening, you can answer this question: "What did God teach me today?"

If you journal in the morning, you can answer this question: "God, what were you trying to teach me yesterday that I missed?" When you reflect on yesterday's events, you may find a common theme that God may have been weaving into your life during the day—one you missed because you were busy. When you see God's hand in your life, even a day later, you know God loves you and is guiding you.

### Record insights from Scripture

Journal about whatever you learn from the Bible. Rewrite a verse in your own words or figure out how a passage is structured. Try to uncover the key truths from the verses and see how the verses apply to your life. (Again, there is no right way to journal. The only wrong way is to not try it at all.)

Intercession (praying behalf on someone else)

supplication (asking for guidance, strength, wisdom.. etc)

adoration

Prayer

confession

ACTSI

thanksgiving

# JOURNAL PAGES

# JOURNAL PAGES

# JOURNAL PAGES

# JOURNAL PAGES

# JOURNAL PAGES

# PRAYING IN YOUR SMALL GROUP

As believers, we're called to support each other in prayer, and prayer should be a consistent part of a healthy small group.

One of prayer's purposes is aligning our hearts with God's. By doing this, we can more easily get in touch with what's at the center of God's heart. Prayer shouldn't be a how-well-did-I-do performance or a self-conscious, put-on-the-spot task to fear. Your small group may need time to get comfortable with praying out loud, too. That's okay.

When you do pray, silently or aloud, follow the practical, simple words of Jesus in Matthew 6:

**Pray sincerely.**

*"And when you pray, do not be like the hypocrites, for they love to pray standing in the synagogues and on the street corners to be seen by men. I tell you the truth, they have received their reward in full." (Matthew 6:5)*

In the Old Testament, God's people were disciplined prayer warriors. They developed specific prayers to use for every special occasion or need. They had prayers for light and darkness, prayers for fire and rain, prayers for good news and bad. They even had prayers for travel, holidays, holy days, and Sabbath days.

Every day the faithful would stop to pray at 9 a.m., noon, and 3 p.m.—a sort of religious coffee break. Their ritual was impressive, to say the least, but being legalistic had its downside. The proud, self-righteous types would strategically plan their schedules to be in the middle of a crowd when it was time for prayer so everyone could hear them as they prayed loudly. You can see the problem. What was intended to promote spiritual passion became a drama to impress others.

God wants our prayers addressed to him alone. That seems obvious enough, yet how many of us pray wanting to impress our listeners rather than wanting to truly communicate with God? This is the problem if you're prideful like the Pharisees about the excellent quality of your prayers. But it can also be a problem if you're new to prayer and are concerned that you don't know how to "pray right." Don't concern yourself with what others think; just talk to God as if you were sitting in a chair next to him.

**Pray simply.**

*"And when you pray, do not keep on babbling like pagans, for they think they will be heard because of their many words. Do not be like them, for your Father knows what you need before you ask him." (Matthew 6:7-8)*

God isn't looking to be dazzled with brilliantly crafted language. Nor is he impressed with lengthy monologues. It's freeing to know that he wants us to keep it simple.

**Pray specifically.**

*"This, then, is how you should pray: 'Our Father in heaven, hallowed be your name, your kingdom come, your will be done on earth as it is in heaven. Give us today our daily bread. Forgive us our debts, as we also have forgiven our debtors. And lead us not into temptation, but deliver us from the evil one." (Matthew 6:9-13)*

What the church has come to call "The Lord's Prayer" is a model of the kind of brief but specific prayers we may offer anytime, anywhere. Look at some of the specific items mentioned:

- Adoration: "hallowed be your name"

- Provision: "your kingdom come...your will be done...give us today our daily bread"

- Forgiveness: "forgive us our debts"

- Protection: "lead us not into temptation"

# PRAYER REQUEST GUIDELINES

Because prayer time is so vital, group members need some basic guidelines for sharing, handling, and praying for prayer requests. Without a commitment from each person to honor these simple suggestions, prayer time can become dominated by one person, an opportunity to gossip, or a never-ending story time. (There are appropriate times to tell personal stories, but this may not be the best time.)

Here are a few suggestions for each group to consider:

### Write down prayer requests.

Each small group member should write down every prayer request on the "Prayer Request" pages provided. When you commit to a small group, you're agreeing to be part of the spiritual community, and that includes praying for one another. By keeping track of prayer requests, you can see how God answers them. You'll be amazed at God's power and faithfulness.

As an alternative, one person can record the requests and e-mail them to the rest of the group. If your group chooses this option, safeguard confidentiality. Be sure personal information isn't compromised. Some people share e-mail accounts with parents or siblings. Develop a workable plan for this option.

### Give everybody an opportunity to share.

As a group, consider the amount of time remaining and the number of people who still want to share. You won't be able to share every thought or detail about a situation.

Obviously if someone experiences a crisis, you may need to focus exclusively on that group member by giving him or her extended time and focused prayer. (However, true crises are infrequent.)

The leader can limit the time by making a comment such as one of the following:

- We have time for everyone to share one praise or request.

- Simply share what to pray for. We can talk in more detail later.

- We're only going to pray for requests about the people in our group. How can we pray for you specifically?

- We've run out of time to share prayer requests. Take a moment to write down your prayer request and give it to me [or identify another person]. You'll get them by e-mail tomorrow.

### Just as people are free to share, they're free to not share.

The goal of a healthy small group should be to create an environment where participants feel comfortable sharing about their lives. Still, not everyone needs to share each week. Here's what I tell my small group:

> As a small group we're here to support one another in prayer. This doesn't mean that everyone has to share something. In fact, don't assume you have to share at all. There's no need to make up prayer requests just to have something to say. If you have something you'd like the group to pray for, let us know. If not, that's fine, too.

### No gossip allowed.

Don't allow sharing prayer requests to become an excuse for gossip. If you're not part of the problem or solution, consider the information gossip. Share the request without the story behind it—that helps prevent gossip. Also speak in general terms without giving names or details ("I have a friend who's in trouble. God knows who it is. Pray for me that I can be a good friend.").

If a prayer request starts going astray, someone should kindly intercede, perhaps with a question such as, "How can we pray for you in this situation?"

### Don't give advice or try to fix the problem.

When people share their struggles and problems, a common response is to try to fix the problem by offering advice. At the right time, the group might provide input on a particular problem, but during prayer time, keep focused on praying for the need. Often God's best work in a person's life comes through times of struggle and pain.

### Keep in touch.

Make sure you exchange phone numbers and e-mail addresses before you leave the first meeting. That way you can contact someone who needs prayer or encouragement before the next time your group meets. You can write each person's contact information on the "Small Group Roster" (page 99).

# PRAYER OPTIONS

There's no single, correct way to end all your sessions. In addition to the options provided in each session, here are some additional ideas.

### During the Small Group Gathering

- One person closes in prayer for the entire group.

- Pray silently. Have one person close the silent prayer time after a while with "amen."

- The leader or another group member prays out loud for each person in the group.

- Everyone prays for one request or person. This can be done randomly during prayer or, as the request is shared, a willing person can announce, "I'll pray for that."

- Everyone who wants to pray takes a turn. Not everyone needs to pray out loud.

- Split the group in half and pray together in smaller groups.

- Pair up and pray for each other.

- On occasion, each person can share what he or she is thankful for before a prayer request, so prayer requests don't become negative from focusing only on problems. Prayer isn't just asking for stuff—it also includes praising God and being thankful for his generosity toward us.

- If you're having an animated discussion about a Bible passage or a life situation, don't feel like you must cut it short for prayer requests. Use it as an opportunity to add a little variety to the prayer time by praying some other day between sessions.

### Outside the Group Time

You can use these options if you run out of time to pray during the meeting or in addition to prayer during the meeting.

- Send prayer requests to each other via e-mail.

- Pick prayer partners and phone each other during the week.

- Have each person in the small group choose a day to pray for everyone in the group. Perhaps you can work it out to have each day of the week covered. Let participants report back at each meeting for accountability.

- Have each person pray for just one other person in the group for the entire week. (Everyone prays for the person on the left or on the right or draw names.)

# PRAYER REQUEST LOG

DATE

NAME

REQUEST

ANSWER

# PRAYER REQUEST LOG

| DATE | NAME | REQUEST | ANSWER |
|------|------|---------|--------|
|      |      |         |        |
|      |      |         |        |
|      |      |         |        |
|      |      |         |        |
|      |      |         |        |
|      |      |         |        |
|      |      |         |        |
|      |      |         |        |
|      |      |         |        |
|      |      |         |        |

# PRAYER REQUEST LOG

| DATE | NAME | REQUEST | ANSWER |
|------|------|---------|--------|
|      |      |         |        |
|      |      |         |        |
|      |      |         |        |
|      |      |         |        |
|      |      |         |        |
|      |      |         |        |
|      |      |         |        |
|      |      |         |        |
|      |      |         |        |
|      |      |         |        |

# PRAYER REQUEST LOG

| DATE | NAME | REQUEST | ANSWER |
|------|------|---------|--------|
|      |      |         |        |

# PRAYER REQUEST LOG

| DATE | NAME | REQUEST | ANSWER |
|------|------|---------|--------|
|      |      |         |        |
|      |      |         |        |
|      |      |         |        |
|      |      |         |        |
|      |      |         |        |
|      |      |         |        |
|      |      |         |        |
|      |      |         |        |
|      |      |         |        |
|      |      |         |        |
|      |      |         |        |

# PRAYER REQUEST LOG

| DATE | NAME | REQUEST | ANSWER |
|------|------|---------|--------|
|      |      |         |        |
|      |      |         |        |
|      |      |         |        |
|      |      |         |        |
|      |      |         |        |
|      |      |         |        |
|      |      |         |        |
|      |      |         |        |
|      |      |         |        |
|      |      |         |        |

# EXPERIENCING CHRIST TOGETHER FOR A YEAR

Your group will benefit the most if you work through the entire EXPE-RIENCING CHRIST TOGETHER series. The longer your group is together, the better your chances of maturing spiritually and integrating the biblical purposes into your life. Here's a plan to complete the series in one year.

Begin with a planning meeting and review the books in the series. They are:

*Book 1—Beginning in Jesus: Six Sessions on the Life of Christ*

*Book 2—Connecting in Jesus: Six Sessions on Fellowship*

*Book 3—Growing in Jesus: Six Sessions on Discipleship*

*Book 4—Serving Like Jesus: Six Sessions on Ministry*

*Book 5—Sharing Jesus: Six Sessions on Evangelism*

*Book 6—Surrendering to Jesus: Six Sessions on Worship*

We recommend you begin with *Book 1—Beginning in Jesus: Six Sessions on the Life of Christ,* because it contains an introduction to six qualities of Jesus. After that, you can use the books in any order that works for your particular ministry.

As you look at your youth ministry calendar, you may want to tailor the order in which you study the books to complement events your youth group will experience. For example, if you plan to have an evangelism outreach, study *Book 5—Sharing Jesus: Six Sessions on Evangelism* first to build momentum. Or study *Book 4—Serving Like Jesus: Six Sessions on Ministry* in late winter to prepare for the spring break missions trip.

Use your imagination and celebrate the completion of each book. Have a worship service, an outreach party, a service project, a fun night out, a meet-the-family dinner, or whatever else you can dream up.

| Number of Weeks | Meeting Topic |
| --- | --- |
| 1 | Planning meeting—a casual gathering to get acquainted, discuss expectations, and refine the covenant (page 18). |
| 6 | Beginning in Jesus: Six Sessions on the Life of Christ |
| 1 | Celebration |
| 6 | Connecting in Jesus: Six Sessions on Fellowship |
| 1 | Celebration |
| 6 | Growing in Jesus: Six Sessions on Discipleship |
| 1 | Celebration |
| 6 | Serving Like Jesus: Six Sessions on Ministry |
| 1 | Celebration |
| 6 | Sharing Jesus: Six Sessions on Evangelism |
| 1 | Celebration |
| 6 | Surrendering to Jesus: Six Sessions on Worship |
| 1 | Celebration |
| 2 | Christmas Break |
| 1 | Easter Break |
| 6 | Summer Break |

# ABOUT THE AUTHORS

A youth ministry veteran of 25 years, **Doug Fields** has authored or co-authored more than 40 books, including *Purpose-Driven® Youth Ministry* and *Your First Two Years in Youth Ministry*. With an M.Div. from Fuller Theological Seminary, Doug is a teaching pastor and pastor to students at Saddleback Church in Southern California and president of Simply Youth Ministry. He and his wife, Cathy, have three children.

**Brett Eastman** has served as the leader of small groups for both Willow Creek Community Church and Saddleback Church. Brett is now the founder and CEO of LIFETOGETHER, a ministry whose mission is to "transform lives through community." Brett earned his masters of divinity degree from Talbot School of Theology and lives in Southern California.

Kids enjoy a fun youth group, but they love a real community even more.

*Experiencing Christ Together* is more than just a year's worth of small group studies—it's a way that students can move closer to God and learn to share his love with each other.

You can help transform your small groups into loving, Christ-centered communities with the tools at your disposal in these 36 lessons and three teaching DVDs.

**Experiencing Christ Together, Student Edition Kit**
12 Sessions on Discovering What Leadership Means for Students Today

Doug Fields and Brett Eastman

RETAIL $129.99
ISBN 0310266424

visit your local Christian bookstore or
www.youthspecialties.com/store

**Youth Specialties**

This 36 session DVD curriculum kit is a totally unique resource for students, built upon the model of the Doing Life Together curriculum for adults (more than 250,000+ study guides sold!)

Doug Fields, the popular and respected youth leader, has written 36 lessons explaining Bible passages and Bible principles, addressing beginning life together, fellowship, discipleship, ministry, evangelism, and worship-teaching, stories, exercises, application points, journaling prompts, and much more!

Brett Eastman and Doug are hosts of the DVDs-each disk are a companion to 2 study guides. You or your small group leaders can "join" conversations to gather hints from the experience of these veteran youth leaders. Plus each DVD includes 12 actual Bible lessons, taped as Doug Fields, Duffy Robbins, Helen Musick, Efrem Smith, Marv

Penner, and Mike Yaconelli unpacking the core lessons and themes. Take away tips on communication or let these experts pinch-hit as leaders for your small group!

Books and DVDs are available individually, but small groups will find it more beneficial to follow the suggested full year outline for the use of all the resources in this one giant kit.

**Life Together, Student Edition**
Doug Fields

RETAIL $129.99
**ISBN 0-310-25332-2**

visit www.youthspecialties.com/store
or your local Christian bookstore

Youth Specialties

You know that being a student leader is no small task—nor is it something to lose sleep over. If you have student leaders—or at least students who are willing to lead—use this book to pair their willingness with tools and techniques to creative effective leaders who lighten your load.

**Help! I'm a Student Leader!**
Practical Ideas and Guidance on Leadership
Doug Fields

RETAIL $9.99
ISBN 0-310-25961-4

visit www.youthspecialties.com/store
or your local Christian bookstore

Youth Specialties